Catalogue of the Collection of maps Prints and Photographs illustrating the history of the Island and City of Bombay

Catalogue of the Collection of maps Prints and Photographs illustrating the history of the Island and City of Bombay

CECIL L. BURNS

GYAN

Published by

Gyan Publishing House
5, Ansari Road
Daryaganj, New Delhi-110002
Phone: 011-47034999, 9811692060
E-mail: books@gyanbooks.com

Distribution Network
gyanbooks.com
India, USA, Canada, UK, Australia, France

ISBN : 978-81-212-9488-1 (PB)
First Published, 1918

2nd Impression 2023

Printed at: Gyan Press, Delhi.

Catalogue of the Collection of Maps Prints and Photographs illustrating the history of the Island and City of bombay
Author:CECIL L. BURNS

CATHARINE OF BRAGANZA, QUEEN OF CHARLES II.

Municipality of Bombay

VICTORIA AND ALBERT MUSEUM, BOMBAY

Catalogue of the Collection of Maps Prints and Photographs illustrating the history of the Island and City of Bombay

BY

CECIL L. BURNS

1918

Contents.

Introduction

THE particular function of a Local, in distinction to that of an Imperial Museum has been the subject of considerable debate among experts in recent years. Before the year 1850 local Museums were almost unknown in England or in India. The original stimulus was given to the movement for their establishment throughout England, by the first International Exhibition in 1851, a movement which soon afterwards spread to India. It lost its early momentum somewhat rapidly, and during the thirty years following its rise the condition of most of these institutions, founded with so much promise of bringing knowledge to, and promoting a taste for beautiful objects among the masses, was somewhat depressing. In England, the scheme was saved from an entire failure by the assistance given to local museums through the excellent system of circulating specimens from the Victoria and Albert Museum at South Kensington. Apart from the works of art thus contributed, the ordinary local museums in England, were neither amusing nor instructive; they were understaffed, inadequately financed, without system, and the galleries in many instances appeared to be the repositories of such articles as the generous donors had no further use for, and wished to get rid of. In recent years a great improvement has taken place, and the true function of the local museum has been more completely realised. Amidst many divergent opinions regarding their sphere of usefulness, ranging from that of a mere raree show to amuse children and the unlearned, to that of a scientist's laboratory, one view met with general accept ance, namely, that each local museum should be a centre for the collection and exhibition of the pictorial and other records, and antiquities connected with the past history of the City and locality in which the museum is situated. Nearly every county in England has its Archæological Society with many enthusiastic antiquarians as members, and it is due to the co-operation between these societies and the Curators of the Museums that the contents of these institutions have become so valuable to students and interesting to the public. Many museums have been fortunate in acquiring by purchase, gift, or bequest, valuable private collections of historical records; the public spirit of local residents having been stimulated by pride in their museums. The most striking example of the results which can be achieved when enthusiasm and expert knowledge are supplemented by private munificence has recently been seen in the foundation of the London Museum, and the furnishing of its galleries with a priceless and unique collection of specimens illustrating the history of that City for over a thousand years. In India most of the drawbacks noticed in English Local Museums were present and are being very slowly remedied. In order to remove one of these, I decided soon after taking charge of the Victoria and Albert Museum to start upon a modest scale a collection of pictorial records of the City and Island of Bombay; and despite the intervention of more urgent duties, this work has been carried on for some years. As occasion has served, maps, plans, prints, books and photographs illustrating the past history of the Island and the City have been acquired. The collection having attained dimensions sufficiently large to warrant its exhibition to the public, the catalogue now issued has been compiled to supplement and explain the pictures on the walls. All that can be claimed for both is that they mark the commencement of a collection of pictorial records, which it is to be hoped will, in course of time, become more comprehensive; and that the existence of this collection will stimulate the interest of the citizens of Bombay in her past history, and induce those who possess historical records to assist in making the collection more perfect in detail.

My thanks are due to Mr. S. T. Sheppard for the gift of several valuable prints, and I am especially indebted to Mr. D. A. Pai, the Assistant Curator of the Museum for the care and labour he has bestowed upon research connected with the catalogue. Mr. Chunilal Murlidhar, the First Assistant has also done excellent work in preparing many of the photographs of existing monuments and in copying pictures when the originals could not be obtained.

CECIL L. BURNS,
Curator and Secretary,
Victoria and Albert Museum.

Charles II, King of England. Natus 1630; Obit 1685.

THE

Island and City of Bombay.

THE generally accepted derivation of the name Bombay is from "Mumbai", the patron deity of the pre-Christian Kolis, the earliest known inhabitants of the Island.

The group of seven islands, which have since been joined so as to form a single island, were included in the Kingdom of Asoka, the famous Maurya Emperor. After his death, they passed into the hands of different Hindu Rulers till the year 1348, when they were conquered by the Muhammadans of Gujrat, and were governed by the kings of that Province for two centuries. The only vestige of their dominion now remaining is the Mosque at Mahim over the tomb of a Muhammadan saint, Makhdam Fakih Ali, who is stated to have died in the year 1431.

About the beginning of the 16th century, the Portuguese who already possessed many of the most important trading centres and cities on the Western Coast of India, came into conflict with the Muhammadan Rulers of the Island, who were forced after some years of active hostilities, to cede Bombay to the Portuguese in the year 1534.

The foundation of the English East India Company in 1600, brought a new power into India. This Company of merchant adventurers was at first permitted only to rent factories in Surat and other places on the Western Coast; but the advantages attendant upon securing and fortifying territory free from the attacks and impositions of Hindu and Muhammadan rulers were so obvious, that as early as 1626 an attempt was made, conjointly with the Dutch to secure a footing on the seven islands of Bombay. This was frustrated by the Portuguese, but in 1661, the object was achieved by including the Island o Bombay as a portion of the marriage dowry of Catherine o: Braganza, upon her marriage with King Charles II of England. The importance of this cession was recognised, and resente i by the Portuguese authorities at Goa, who protested vehemently against it, and placed so many obstacles in the way of its fulfilment that nearly five years elapsed between the signing of the treaty and the delivery of the islands. Pepys notes in his Diary on the 15th May 1663: "The Portugals have choused us, it seems, in the Island of Bombay, in the East Indies, for after a great charge of our fleets being sent thither with full commission from the King of Portugal to receive it, the Governor by some pretence or other will not deliver it to Sir Abraham Shipman, sent from the King, nor to my Lord of Marlborough, which the King takes highly ill, and I fear our Queen will fare worse for it." The Islands were handed over in 1666 but their importance failed to impress the British Government, Bombay being described by Pepys as "but a poor little island"; and two years afterwards the new acquisition was leased to the East India Company at a yearly rental of £10.

Sir George Oxenden was the first Governor appointed by the Company. He was succeeded by Mr. Gerald Aungier in the year 1669, whose administration was remarkable for the efforts he made to attract the trading population of both the coast and the interior. He succeeded so well in this, that he was enabled to hand over to his successor a settlement "far more populous, more strongly fortified, better governed than it had been in 1668." In the year 1675, Mr. Aungier left Bombay for Surat, and the next forty years was a period of stagnation and retrogression due in a great measure to the unhealthy condition of the settlement.

The inroads of the sea through the breaches at Mahaluxmi, Worli, and Mahim, which turned the ground between the Islands into swamps, and the insanitary condition of the settlement made it so unhealthy, that Bombay received the name of the "Charnel house in which two monsoons were the age of a man".

During this period the settlement was in constant danger of attack and blockade both by sea and land at the hands of the Muhammadans, the Seedees and the Marathas, owing to the refusal of the Directors of the East India Company in England to provide funds necessary for the provision of adequate fortifications or armament. This danger was averted, and during the Governorship of Charles Boone (1715-1722) the town wall was completed.

During the next forty years, measures were adopted to improve the sanitary condition of the Island. Reclamation works were started to stop the rush of the sea water through the great breach at Mahaluxmi; communications with the neighbouring parts of the mainland were improved; allotments of new lands for building purposes were made; and the construction of buildings outside the fort walls was encouraged. The effect of these efforts and their continuance was seen in a decrease in mortality, and an increase in population and trade. They had important results in altering the topography of the Islands. The construction of the Hornby Vellard completed in the year 1784 during the Governorship of Mr. Hornby, made the wide area of flats available for cultivation and settlement, and joined the eastern and western sides of the Island into one area. In the year 1803, the Island was connected with Salsette by a causeway constructed at Sion. After the deposition of the Peshwa in the year 1818, and the annexation of the Deccan, the work of bringing Bombay into closer touch with the mainland, and of constructing roads and public buildings was carried out with great vigour under the direction of the Hon'ble Mountstuart Elphinstone. The Island of Colaba was joined to Bombay in the year 1838 by a causeway, and seven years later another causeway was constructed at Mahim, which joined the north-western end of Bombay Island to Salsette. By the year 1860, the town had gradually crept over the reclaimed lands, northward of the City; and westward along Back Bay. The appointment of Sir Bartle Frere as Governor of Bombay in the year 1862 synchronised with the rise of the modern city of Bombay, a work in which he took a prominent part.

Bombay had been already brought into close contact with the mainland by the opening of the Great Indian Peninsula and the Bombay, Baroda and Central India Railway Companies in the year 1860. A regular service of coasting steamers between Bombay and the sea ports of Western India was opened in the year 1869, and the opening of the Suez Canal brought about a phenomenal change in the carrying trade of the Island between the East and West. The outbreak of the Civil War in America in the year 1861, caused an enormous increase in the cotton trade of the Island, which resulted in the gain of a huge sum of money estimated at 75 millions sterling. This acquisition of abundant wealth in the hands of the people led to wild speculation. Bubble companies of every description were floated, the shares in which were inflated to extravagant prices, while banks and other financial concerns were started without capital or experience to back or guide their operations. The crash which followed, was a severe set-back to Bombay, but before this came to pass, a portion of the new wealth was devoted to carrying out schemes calculated to improve the City, and to make it more wholesome.

One of the greatest improvements was embodied in the decision of Government to remove the fort walls and to utilise a portion of the space thus set free, for roads, open spaces, and the sites of public buildings, the remainder being sold to the public for building plots. Reclamations on the eastern and western shores of the Island were undertaken; the entire foreshore north and south of the Apollo Bunder was reclaimed and on the western shore, the Back Bay Reclamation between Colaba and Malabar Hill was carried out.

When these reclamations had been completed, the area of the whole Island was increased from 18 to 22 square miles; while the construction of new roads, the widening of the old ones and the erection of great public buildings entirely transformed the City from a mean and cramped collection of houses to one of the finest cities of the empire. The water supply was provided for and secured, and a comprehensive drainage scheme was commenced, which rendered a large area of the low-lying land at the north of the City available for habitation.

The year 1870 was marked by the creation of the Bombay Port Trust charged with the administration of the harbour and wharves, and improvement of the whole foreshore of the City. Its earliest work was the construction of the Prince's Dock, the foundation stone of which was laid by H. R. H. The Prince of Wales (The late King Edward VII) in the year 1875. This took five years to complete, and was followed by the construction of the Victoria Dock and the Merewether Dry Dock which were opened in the year 1888 and 1891 respectively. The foundation stone of the New Alexandra Dock was laid by H. M. The King Emperor in the year 1905, and the Dock was opened by the Viceroy, Lord Hardinge, in March 1914.

The last years of the 19th century were ones of tragic significance to the City occasioned by the appearance and spread of Bubonic Plague, which in the early years of its visitation created great havoc among the inhabitants. The great destruction of human life it caused impressed upon the authorities the need for some systematic improvement of the City, by the opening of congested areas. In order to effect these improvements, the City Improvement Trust was created in the year 1898 and many new streets have been cut through the City, while a great scheme for the creation of a residential quarter in the northern portion of the Island is now in course of development.

Maps of Bombay.

No. 1. (*a*) DAVIES' SKETCH MAP OF BOMBAY HARBOUR, 1626.

This map is reduced from the sketch made by Davies, an English navigator, who participated in the joint attack made on the Island of Bombay by the English and the Dutch on the 13th October 1626. Sir Henry Morland writes: "The sketch appears to have been made from a point off Worlee." It possesses special interest as illustrating the first recorded visit of English ships to the Island of Bombay.

(*b*) FRYER'S MAP OF BOMBAY, 1672.

Dr. John Fryer, M.D. (1650-1733), an enterprising and observant traveller, was Surgeon to the East India Company. He visited Bombay in 1674 and his "New Account of East India and Persia" was published in 1698. Mr. James Douglas in his volume on "Bombay and Western India" points out that the Mahim woods and the fishing stakes in the harbour were at that time precisely where they are at present.

No. 2. (*a*) MAP OF THE ISLAND AND PORT OF BOMBAY WITH THE ADJACENT ISLANDS, 1724.

This map seems to have been prepared by the author of "A Description of the Fort and Island of Bombay in 1724". Here the anchorage for ships in winter is marked as being near to Thana.

(*b*) GROSE'S PLAN OF BOMBAY, 1750.

Mr. Grose was a Writer and a Covenanted Servant of the East India Company. He came to Bombay in the year 1750 in one of the East Indiamen and published his account "Voyages to the East Indies" in two parts in 1772. The plan is invaluable for every street within the walls is laid down and is accompanied by a scale of feet.

View of Bombay from Esplanade, 1670.

View of Bombay from Harbour, 1670.

(*c*) FRENCH PLAN OF BOMBAY FORT, 1758.

This was obtained from Pondicherry by Mr. G. W. Forrest, Officer in charge of the Records of the Government of India, and seems to have been prepared to assist an intended invasion of the Island by the French at about that period.

No. 3. (*a*) NIEBUHR'S MAP, 1764.

Carston Neibuhr, (1733-1815,) was for six months in Bombay in 1763 and has given us some interesting details of the people of that time. He visited the Island of Elephanta and also Surat, where he was much struck with the magnitude of the trade of the place. The chief interest of the map is that it marks the sites of all the Forts from Rewa and Sion to Mazagon and Dongri. It also shows the Castle, on the Tank Bastion of which flies the British Flag.

(*b*) FRENCH PLAN OF BOMBAY ISLAND, 1767.

This was obtained from Pondicherry by Mr. G. W. Forrest.

(*c*) BOMBAY FORT, 1771-1864.

The Bombay Fort, according to Dr. Fryer, was a pretty and well situated house standing on the site of the existing Bombay Castle. It was very weakly fortified, four brass canons being its whole defence. On the English taking possession of the Island, they mounted 120 pieces of ordnance here and in another convenient place 20 more to resist an invasion of the Sidees. Gerald Aungier (1669-1675) for the purpose of protecting the harbour and securing the safety of the population, started the work of surrounding the eastern and western foreshore with ramparts in the year 1675. The work after being unfinished for forty years was continued by Charles Boone, and by the year 1716 a chain of fortifications was completed, north, south, east and west of the Town of Bombay. The remains of these forts may still be seen at Sion, Worli and Mahim and elsewhere. Bombay Fort which was the pivot of these fortifications, extended from Apollo Bunder to a little south of the present site of St. George's Hospital, following more or less the line now taken by Hornby Road. St. George's bastion, the last remnant of which is still to be seen on the eastern frontage of St. George's

Hospital on the Frere Road, was an isolated work and was erected at a somewhat later date.

No. 4. MAP OF BOMBAY AND DISTRICT PREPARED FOR THE PESHWA BY THE PESHWA'S AGENT IN BOMBAY ABOUT 1770.

The Peshwa referred to is Madhavrao (1716-1772). This map appears to have been made before the outbreak of the 1st Marātha war.

No. 5. PLAN OF BOMBAY HARBOUR.

Dedicated to the Hon'ble Jonathan Duncan, Governor of Bombay (1795-1811). This was engraved by James Horsburg.

No. 6. (*a*) THE ISLAND OF BOMBAY.

This map was made in order to extend the survey operations to all parts of the Island with the object of defining the boundaries and extent of the Hon'ble East India Company's property, and that of the inhabitants in general, and for the purpose of specifying the nature of the tenures of all lands in the Island. The survey was commenced under Capt. Dickinson, one of the Company's Engineers in 1812, assisted by Capt. Remon and Lieuts. Jopp and Tate.

(*b*) PLAN OF BOMBAY, COLABA AND SION.

Mr. Douglas in his "Western India" remarks "these maps are the best for accuracy and execution."

No. 7. THE ISLAND OF BOMBAY (SHOWING RECLAMATIONS BETWEEN 1816-1890).

The first important reclamation was the construction of the Vellard in 1784. After this had been completed, the central portions of the Island and flats became available for reclamation, a work which was gradually carried out during the first half of the nineteenth century. The next important reclamation was on the eastern foreshore, when a portion of the sea beach, between Wadi Bandar and Chinch Bunder measuring 1,800 feet long by 300 feet wide was reclaimed in 1865. Other parts of the eastern foreshore were reclaimed from the sea between that date and 1885, when the Docks were commenced. The construction of these led the way to further extensive reclamations. A great scheme was started for the reclamation of Back Bay in 1865, but this was abandoned in consequence of the panic in the Share Market which followed the close of the Civil War in America. The demolition of the ramparts of the Fort in 1862 enabled Government to fill up the *moat* on their outer side towards the Esplanade, and upon this site, Esplanade Road and Hornby Road were made. Since that date the Municipality has reclaimed a considerable portion of the present area of Tardeo and Mahaluxmi, while the Improvement Trust has recently reclaimed a small portion of the southern end of Back Bay upon which now stands Cuffe Parade.

No. 8. FORT OF BOMBAY, 1863.

No. 9. MAP OF THE EAST INDIES AND THE ADJACENT COUNTRIES WITH THE SETTLEMENTS, FACTORIES AND TERRITORIES, EXPLAINING WHAT BELONGS TO ENGLAND, SPAIN, FRANCE, HOLLAND, DENMARK, PORTUGAL, ETC.

Dedicated to the Directors of the Hon'ble United East India Company. Drawn by H. Moll, Esq.

No. 10. FIRE IN BOMBAY ON 17TH FEBRUARY, 1803.

The fire originated in the populous portion of the Bazar in the Fort on the afternoon of 17th February 1803 and raged for nearly a day. Almost one-third of the Town was destroyed. The total number of houses destroyed was 471 and together with the destruction of other property occasioned a loss of about 40 lacs ; there was no loss of life.

Drawn by Lieut.-Col. J. Blank, Acting Chief Engineer.

No. 11. DESCRIPTION OF THE NEW EMPIRE OF MALABAR, CANARA, DECCAN AND OTHER PROVINCES.

From P. Baldaeus' "Description of East India, Coasts of Malabar and Coromandel."

P. Baldaeus visited Malabar and Coromandel about 1649 and was for long a resident in Ceylon. He died in 1671.

No. 12. GOA.

From P. Baldaeus' "Description of East India, Coasts of Malabar and Coromandel."

No. 13. MAP OF THE ISLAND OF BOMBAY.

A reduced copy of Col. Laughton's map of 1872.

This map was prepared under orders from the Government of India by the Revenue Survey Department under Col. Laughton. The Survey was commenced in November 1865 and finished in November 1872. It is pronounced by experts to be most accurate and complete.

No. 14. RELIEF MAP OF BOMBAY 1666.

This relief map shows the general contours of the seven islands comprising Bombay when they were first taken over by the British. It will be seen that the whole of the central area north of the Island upon which the Fort was erected, was a swamp caused by the influx of the sea at various points, and this map illustrates the information given under the heading of the "Island and City of Bombay."

No. 15. RELIEF MAP OF BOMBAY, 1914.

This map further illustrates the information given under the heading of the "Island and City of Bombay" and shows the changes which have taken place due to the closing of the breaches which formerly allowed the sea to flood the central portion of the Island, and the increase in the area due to various reclamations.

Views of Bombay and other British Settlements on the Western Coast of India in the 17th Century.

No. 16. THE CITY OF AMADABATH.

A print taken from "East India and Ceylon" by P. Baldaeus, 1649.

No. 17. SURATTE.

A print taken from "East India and Ceylon" by P. Baldaeus, 1649.

No. 18. (*a*) VIEW OF BOMBAY FORT, FROM ESPLANADE, 1670.
(*b*) VIEW OF BOMBAY FROM HARBOUR, 1670.

"Here the Portuguese having built a very fine Castle." P. Baldaeus', "East India and Ceylon."

No. 19. (*a*) THE SOUTH VIEW OF SURAT CASTLE.
(*b*) THE WEST VIEW OF SURAT CASTLE.
(*c*) THE EAST VIEW OF SURAT CASTLE.

This Castle was built about 1650 upon the bank of the river Tapti, and is thus described by Mr. Grose, a Writer and Covenanted servant of the East India Company in his "Voyage to the East Indies." "It appears a strange bundle of buildings, fortified with canon mounted here and there, without order and meaning, and without an attempt at anything like military architecture."

Views of Bombay in the 18th Century.

No. 20. (*a*) THE WEST SIDE OF BOMBAY GREEN IN 1750.

St. Thomas' Church and Church Gate in the distance.

Grose in his "Voyage to the East Indies" writes as follows: "The only English Church at Bombay, and which is full sufficient for any possible congregation of them as it is, is a building extremely neat, commodious and airy, being situate on what is called the Green."

(*b*) TODDY TREE.

Mrs. Postans in her "Western India 1838" writes: "The plantations of cocoanut trees are very valuable for the fermented juice called Toddy which forms an intoxicating liquor in great demand amongst the natives. The Bhandarees or Toddy-drawers climb the trees with the aid of notches cut in the bark and on reaching the tufted crown of foliage, tie up the "embryo bud" to prevent its expansion, and then making a small incision at the end, let the juice ooze out in gentle drops into large earthen jars, which are fastened over the incision and left to hang all night on the trees. When fresh, the liquor is pleasant to taste, but when fermented, does not appeal to western taste."

(*c*) BOATS OFF THE MALABAR COAST.

From a picture drawn by W. Daniel,.Esq., R.A.

Gilbert in his "India illustrated" describes these boats as follows: "These boats are of singular construction having generally a high poop, and being remarkably low at the bows, though some of them are flush fore and aft, carrying large sails, which expose them to great danger when overtaken by sudden squalls. They are sluggish sailors and in calm weather are urged forward by the oars. The number of men employed to navigate them is from twenty to thirty according to size. They are so loosely put together that their seams open and admit so large a quantity of water, as often to endanger the safety not only of the cargo but of the crew. In stormy weather, their commanders seldom venture out of sight of land, as these vessels are not constructed for weathering severe gales. They have however a very pictureque appearance, when seen coasting along the shore of Malabar, freighted with cargo from Arabia or Persia."

No. 21. (*a*) View of Bombay from Malabar Hill with the Island of Karanja and part of the Indian Continent in the distance, 1772.

(*b*) View of Bombay Green, 1768, taken from the Writers' apartment at the Bundar.

(*c*) View of Bombay, taken from the Harbour in 1773.

These three views are very valuable, as they show the appearance of Bombay in Mr. Forbes' time. The first view was taken from Malabar Hill in the year 1772; the second, was taken in the year 1768 from the roof of the Custom House, where Mr. Forbes then lived, from which a look-out in those days was obtained without interruption to the Cathedral and Government House in Apollo Street. The carriage of His Excellency Governor Hodges, drawn by four horses and preceded by a dozen horn blowers and Bhandarins, is a conspicuous object in this picture. The third is taken from the sea in the year 1773.

Mr. James Forbes came as a Writer in the East India Company's service to Bombay in 1765 and finally returned to England in 1784. He is the author of the well-known book "Forbes' Oriental Memoirs" published in 1812, which was founded on a series of letters written during his residence in India.

No. 22. A view of the Island of Bombay and Salsette.

With surrounding country, taken from an elevated position.

The engraving is inscribed as follows "To Sir Charles Warre Malet, Bart., this print from the original picture in his possession is (by permission) dedicated by his much obliged and obedient servant, Rob. Cribb."

Published in June 1803, *engraved by T. S. Barth.*

Sir C. W. Malet, Bart., (1752-1815,) was a Bombay Civilian and arrived in Western India in 1770. He was a great sportsman, and took part in the first great lion hunt at Ahmedabad in 1781. In 1785, at the request of Nana Phadnavis, he was appointed Resident at the Court of the Peshwa, and in this capacity had the honour of being received by the Peshwa in the Grand Durbar in 1790. He left India soon after 1799, and it was to him that Mr. Forbes dedicated his "Oriental Memoirs."

No. 23. The fleet under convoy of H. M's Ship "Chiffone", Capt. Wainright, leaving Bombay Harbour on September 14th, 1809, from the Apollo Gate.

Published, April 1813.

The Bombay Government issued orders in the year 1809, to relieve the Imam of Muscat from the power of the Wahabees, and at the same time to suppress the Joasmi pirates. For this purpose an expedition proceeded to the Persian Gulf. The naval portion assembled at Bombay under the Command of Commodore T. Wainright, and consisted of H. M. ships "Chiffone" and "Caroline," each carrying thirty-six guns, which convoyed ten transports with troops and stores. The fleet reached Muscat, and after a brief interview with the Imam, it was decided to attack Ras-ul-Khymah, the capital city of the Joasmi, which was taken by the British in November 1809. The fleet returned to Bombay in 1810.

No. 24. "Bombay on the Malabar Coast belonging to the East India Company, 1665-1700."

Published on the 12*th of May* 1794, *according to an Act of Parliament, and drawn by T. Van Ryne.*

This print was made after the painting by John Bowles which hung in the Court Room of the East India Company's House in Leaden Hall Street, London.

Church Gate, with the Walls in Course of Demolition, 1862.

Views of Bombay in the 19th Century.

No. 25. (*a*) THE GREEN WITH THE TOWN HALL AND MINT ABOUT 1850.

THE GREEN. The original Cotton Green of Bombay, was known as the Bombay Green and occupied the area between the Old Secretariat on the south, the entrance to Bazar Gate on the north, the Town Hall on the east, and the Cathedral and Church Gate Street on the west. In 1813, the open area was covered with cotton bales and other merchandise. Around the Green were various public offices and on an enclosed portion stood the statue of Lord Cornwallis under a masonry canopy.

THE TOWN HALL. In the early years of the British rule, the City of Bombay possessed no Town Hall. In the year 1675, a hired house in which judicial courts were located was used as a Town Hall, and in 1677 one of the rooms in the Court House of Gerald Aungier was called the Town Hall. In 1720 a house belonging to a private citizen one Rama Kamat and in 1786 a room in Hornby House (now the Great Western Hotel) were used for the like purpose. Proposals for erecting a special building were first made in the year 1793, but nothing appears to have been done till 1811, when the project was again brought forward by Sir J. Mackintosh. In 1812 Government accepted the scheme, and an attempt was made to raise the funds required by means of three lotteries held under official sanction. The money collected by this means was not sufficient to complete the building, and further private subscriptions not being forthcoming, Government took the work in hand and the building, was finished in 1833 at a total cost of a little more than six lacs. The building as it now stands, was designed by Col. Cowper, R.E., the original plans having been considerably modified. Its plan includes a main hall and two wings. The main hall has a fine entrance porch surmounted by a pediment supported by Doric columns. The approach to the entrance is by a flight of steps which form an impressive feature in the facade. The doorways to the northern and southern wings each lead to a separate vestibule, containing a circular staircase giving access to broad landings upon which the doorways leading to the main hall and the various rooms open. The main hall is 88 feet long by 85 feet 6 inches broad, the coved ceiling being supported by detached pillars of Corinthian design. At the northern end is a muscians' gallery, while the southern end is occupied by a platform and organ ; this organ was presented by Sir A. Sassoon in 1872. It is a fine instrument upon which a considerable sum has been expended in recent years. The proportions of the main hall and the adjoining rooms are excellent and the whole building though somewhat severe in character, is considered by many experts to be unexcelled for dignity by any in the City. The building contains some fine statues of past Governors, and public men. The main hall is used for public meetings of a non-political character, for concerts and exhibitions. The northern wing of the building is occupied by the Library and offices of the Royal Asiatic Society, and the southern wing and basement by the offices of the Collector of Bombay. The Durbar Room, adjoining the main hall, was used for the meetings of the Bombay Legislative Council, and for Levies held by the Governor of Bombay before the present Secretariat building was erected.

The Mint (about 1850). The minting of coins in Bombay was commenced in the year 1670 in the old mint established by Mr. Gerald Aungier, and was continued in a building somewhere near the Town Barracks and the Castle. The present building was commenced in 1824 from designs by Major John Hawkins of the Bombay Engineers and was completed in 1829.

(*b*) The Green, Custom House and Harbour, 1850.

The Custom House and Harbour, 1850: From the year 1665 to 1714, the English Custom House was situated at Mody Bay, and formed part of what was then known as the East India House (see print No. 24). The chief Bunder or Landing place was at some distance from this house, probably on the spot where the Custom House now stands. About the year 1710, Governor Aislabie ordered the erection of warehouses near the chief Bunder, and these formed the nucleus of the present Custom Office. These warehouses, as also the entire facade of the building, were completed about the year 1714, as recorded by the inscription on a slab placed over the porch, "The Honourable Aislabie, Esq. 1714" under the Coat of Arms of the East India Company. Originally the warehouses consisted of rows of buildings parallel to the street front, but about the year 1758 they were altered to provide accommodation for the Company's covenanted servants. The alterations took the form of two buildings at each end of the Bunder, which to-day form the wings of the Custom House. It was in one of these houses that Mr. Forbes lived when a young writer in the Company's service. About the year 1802, the front row of houses was turned into the Custom House; this block was enlarged in 1840, at the instance of the merchants and Chamber of Commerce, and again in 1895, to give increased accommodation for offices and staff of the Customs Department.

(*c*) The Bombay Green, now Elphinstone Circle.

(*For "The Bombay Green" see note on 'a'.*)

In the year 1844, the Agri-Horticultural Society commenced making a flower garden on the Green, but definite alterations did not take place till 1863, when Mr. Forjet, the Police Commissioner, conceived the idea of converting the portion in front of the Town Hall into a Circle. Lord Elphinstone and Sir B. Frere warmly supported the idea and by 1865, the buildings, comprising this Circle named according to the unanimous wish of the leading citizens after Lord Elphinstone, were completed and ready for occupation.

No. 26. PLAN OF THE TOWN HALL.

No. 27. VIEW OF A PART OF BOMBAY GREEN, BETWEEN 1811 and 1826.

The buildings represented are the Church, and the Counting House of Messrs. Forbes & Co. The three figures in the right middle foreground are intended to represent Armenians, two of them being merchants and the third a priest.

Drawn some time between 1811 and 1826 by Capt. Grindley and engraved by R. G. Reeve for Grindley's "Indian Scenery."

No. 28. VIEW OF A PART OF BOMBAY TAKEN FROM THE BOMBAY GREEN, 1811 AND 1826.

This is another view of Bombay drawn by the same artist. The buildings in front are the offices of the Secretary to Government, which were subsequently used as the Court of Sadar Adalut, a Supreme Court of Appeal of the East India Company's Judicial Establishment. The building on the right is the old theatre.

This theatre was originally built by public subscription in 1770, but in course of time fell into such a state of disrepair that in the year 1819, it had to be renovated by a grant sanctioned by Government. It was finally sold about the year 1836 by Government.

Drawn by Capt. Grindley and engraved by R. E. Reeve for Grindley's "Indian Scenery."

No. 29. A VIEW OF BOMBAY, 1831.

(*The Original was painted by R. Burford.*)

This view is taken from Mazagon Hill, a short distance from what was then known as the Black Town. It embraces a considerable portion of this part of the town, the immediate foreground being occupied by singularly constructed and curiously ornamented villas on the sides of Mazagon Hill, and the pleasant village of the same name at its base. Towards the south-east stretches the Black Town and Esplanade, the Fort of Bombay forming the extreme point. Towards the north, a constant succession of villas and cottages occupy

View of a part of Bombay taken from the Bombay Green between 1811-1826.

sites adjoining the beach, while towards the east the Harbour is seen, whose smooth expanse is broken here and there by wooded islands, to which the Ghauts and the mountains of the mainland form a striking background.

No. 30. Lord Wellesley's Monument in Bombay.

(*Now erected in the Elphinstone Circle Garden.*)

This monument was erected by the public after Lord Wellesley's departure. The Statue is the work of Chantrey. For some years after its arrival in Bombay it lay neglected in the warehouse of Messrs. Forbes and Co., but through the exertions and a liberal contribution made by Sir Charles Forbes, it was eventually placed in its present position.

The Marquis of Wellesley (1760-1842) was educated at Eton and Oxford. He entered the House of Commons in 1784, and was made a Member of the Board of Control over Indian affairs in 1793. He was appointed Governor-General of India in 1797. His term of office was marked by successful wars against Tipu of Mysore in 1799 and against Scindia and the Raja of Berar in 1803. He founded a College at Fort William. before leaving India in 1805.

No. 31. (*a*) Bombay Architecture before the time of Sir Bartle Frere.

Site of Bazar Gate after demolition.

(*b*) Memorial to a Parsee Ship-Builder.

Erected to the memory of Bomonji Hormasji Wadia, Esq., J.P., by public subscription in 1880.

(*c*) Fort with newly planted avenue on the Esplanade.

This avenue was planted in 1857 and ran from that part of the Esplanade opposite Churchgate to Kalbadevi.

No. 32. (*a*) Colaba Causeway 1840.

The Causeway was built in the year 1838, and widened and rebuilt in 1861-63. Colaba was a pleasant and retired residential quarter, cut off at high tide from the Island of Bombay. Before this Causeway was built, the roadway was so difficult to negotiate that occasionally persons were drowned in attempting to cross the channel.

(*b*) Dockyard Building, from the Road.

The commencement of the Dockyard dates from about the year 1670, when under orders from the Directors of the East India Company, a naval architect, Mr. W. Pitt, was sent out to construct two vessels for the defence of the port and to impart instruction to the Indians in the art of ship-building. This was followed by the removal from Surat to Bombay of all the marine forces of the Company. In the beginning the Dock was a sort of mud basin, on the spot where the docks are now situated, in and out of which the tide flowed at will, and it was not until about 1735, that this primitive dock was improved; when one Lowji Wadia, who showed remarkable aptitude for ship-building, with other Parsee shipwrights, was persuaded to come to Bombay. They commenced their work with great activity, which was further stimulated by the construction of a proper dry-dock. In 1748, Governor Wake decided to have a dock built at a cost of Rs. 5,000. Under Governor Bourchier the dock was lengthened. In 1754, Government sanctioned the building of a second dock in a line with the first which was completed in 1762 at a cost of Rs. 12,000, and in 1765, a third dock was completed under Governor Crommelin. In 1804, at the request of the Admiral for a larger dock, it was decided to build a new dock, but it was not till 1807 that work was commenced and on the New Year's Day of 1808, the dock was opened by Governor Duncan.

The Government Dockyard has been engaged in fitting out many expeditions. Here fleets were prepared against the Angrias, the French and the Portuguese in the seventeenth and eighteenth centuries, while in later years, expeditions to the Persian Gulf, the Red Sea, Abyssinia, Burmah, China and the Cape have been largely indebted to the Bombay Dockyard for the supply of transports. It is the principal dockyard for the repair of H. M.'s ships on the East Indian Station. Among the many notable men who have passed through its gates may be mentioned the Duke of Wellington in 1801 and Lord Nelson.

(c) THE NEW PIER OF THE DOCKYARD.

No. 33. (a) CHURCH GATE SHOWING RECLAMATION WORK FOR THE B. B. & C. I. RAILWAY STATION AND OFFICES, 1864.

This site was chosen by Sir S. Fitzgerald. The work of reclaiming land from the sea has greatly contributed to render Bombay "healthy and habitable." The idea of reclaiming submerged land had previously occupied the minds of the Portuguese authorities; while after the transfer of the Island from the Crown to the East India Company, the Court of Directors ordered their representatives at Bombay to encourage speculators to stop the breaches through which the sea overflowed. In the beginning only small tracts of land here and there were reclaimed, no serious effort to check the inroad of the sea being made till the year 1784, when the Hornby Vellard was completed. On the completion of the Vellard, the central portions of the Island and the Flats were gradually filled in and raised. In the beginning reclamations on a small scale were taken in hand ; but by the year 1855, a considerable area of land in the interior of the Island had been reclaimed. The main effort to reclaim the foreshores was made after 1860. With the accumulation of wealth in the hands of the people, due to the outbreak of the American Civil War, many Companies for reclaiming portions of land were started and these alone or in conjunction with Government, carried out the Apollo Bunder, Mody Bay, Elphinstone, Mazagon, Tank Bundar, and Frere Reclamations on the east side of the Island ; and the Back Bay Reclamation from Colaba to the foot of the Malabar Hill on the western side. By the end of the year 1866, about 470 acres of land were reclaimed on the eastern foreshore. Meanwhile work had been proceeding at the Apollo Bundar where it was arranged to reclaim about 20 acres of land, but subsequently in order to provide room for the B. B. & C. I.

Railway Company, it became necessary to reclaim more land. The Back Bay Reclamation Company, which had already been established, decided upon the ambitious project of reclaiming the whole of the Bay, but in the year 1865, on account of the collapse of credit following the share mania. the Company had to go into liquidation, and the scheme was abandoned. Government ultimately reclaimed just so much land as was necessary for a ride and a footpath along the sea shore, for the railway lines of the B. B. & C. I. Railway and a carriage road (Queen's Road) which now represents roughly the original line of the foreshore.

The demolition of the ramparts enabled Government to fill up old ditches and hollows on the Esplanade, while the Bombay Municipality took in hand the partial reclamation of the Flats with town sweepings, and the filling up of old tanks and quarries.

The Bombay Port Trust since its creation in the year 1873, has carried out extensive reclamations on the eastern foreshore amounting to nearly 165 acres. In the year 1907, the great Mazagon Reclamation Scheme was commenced, its foundation stone being laid by H. E. Lord Sydenham, the Governor of Bombay, in the month of December of that year. The total area to be reclaimed by the operations of this scheme is about 583 acres, at an estimated cost of nearly 157 lacs of rupees. On the completion of the scheme. it is proposed to transfer the Cotton Green from Colaba to Mazagon, where it will be located on a more spacious site. It is also proposed to transfer the whole of the grain and seed trade to this site and a harbour railway from Sion and a branch line from Mahim have already been opened for traffic.

Another reclamation was completed by the City Improvement Trust in 1906 at Colaba (known as Cuffe Parade) which has rendered available for residential purposes, about 90,000 square yards of the foreshore of Back Bay. This project was completed at a cost of nearly 5 lacs and has proved so lucrative that the desirability of reclaiming further areas on the Back

Bay is at present engaging the attention of the authorities.

(*b*) THE NEW PRONG'S LIGHT HOUSE.

This light house is situated one and one-fifth of a mile south of Colaba. It took the place of an older light house, the remains of which can still be seen on the Island of Colaba. The light can be seen eighteen miles by an observer from the sea. It was erected to guard the Prong's Reef. There are eight rooms in the light house for the staff and for use as store rooms. The light shows a bright flash every ten seconds. This is one of the largest light houses in the world. It cost £60,000.

(*c*) THE OLD LIGHT HOUSE, COLABA.

This light house was built in the year 1768 and superseded the Signal House erected on Old Woman's Island in 1766. It was completed at a cost of Rs. 5,000. In 1797, the Court of Directors sent out a new frame of lamps and reflectors, for the accommodation of which, a new lantern was constructed by the Bombay Government at a cost of Rs. 6,653. It was 150 feet in height above the sea level and its light was visible for seven miles at sea in clear weather.

No. 34. (*a*) ESPLANADE ROAD.

This view was taken about the year 1864. The laying out of the Esplanade Road was made possible by the demolition of the Fort walls which took place between the years 1862 and 1865.

(*b*) BELVEDERE HOUSE, MAZAGON.

This is also called "Mazagon House," by Mrs. Ellwood, an early traveller in India. It was a handsome old fashioned building situated on Mazagon Hill overlooking the harbour, and was formerly part of a Portuguese Convent. Here lived Mrs. Eliza Draper to whom the "Letters from Yorick," published in 1775, were addressed by Laurence Sterne. It was still standing in 1864, according to Dr. A. Leith, and was used for many years as the P. & O. Club.

No. 35. (*a*) CHURCH GATE AND RAMPARTS IN 1820.

This photograph is taken from a drawing made by W. Westall, A.R.A., and engraved by R. G. Reeve. It represents the western extremity of the Fort commanding the approach from the western and northern part of the Island.

(*b*) REMAINS OF OLD BOMBAY.

In the compound of St. George's Hospital.

(*c*) THE BAZAR GATE SHORTLY BEFORE DEMOLITION.

This Gate stood exactly on the spot where now stands the Bazar Gate Police Station, and was situated on the northern side of the Fort. It was a great gate and served as a protection and gave access to that portion of the Fort, which was thickly populated.

No. 36. (*a*) BOMBAY CASTLE FROM WITHIN.

Bombay Castle is a quadrangle, and has an area of about 20,903 square yards. Amongst other interesting memorials of antiquity which it contains, is the Sun Dial (shown in (*c*)), the Arsenal Weighing Book, in which the names of a great many Bombay Officers appear with their respective weights, from about the year 1808, and a great Portuguese bell which from the inscription thereon appears to have been cast about the year 1674. It also contains a great dungeon which was used in early years as the Prison House.

(*b*) THE OLD GATE OF BOMBAY CASTLE.

This lofty gate was built by the Portuguese. The two figures represent Portuguese soldiers in their trunkhose, bearing aloft the great globe signifying the idea of Portuguese dominion by sea and land.

(*c*) THE SUN DIAL IN BOMBAY CASTLE.

This is ten feet high and is embellished with much grotesque carving, including heads of men, monsters, and animals intermingled with leaves towering high above the dial face. The marking of the hours is still distinctly visible. This is the oldest sculptured work in Bombay belonging to the period of the Portuguese occupation.

A Relic of Portuguese Occupation—The Sun-dial in Bombay Castle.

The Ramparts and Look-out Tower, Bombay Castle

No. 37. (*a*) APOLLO GATE IN 1862.

This gate was probably the last portion of the wall to be completed, for a stone taken out of it in the year 1857 contained the following inscription : " The Town Wall was finished in the year 1716, when Charles Boone was Governor." It was situated not far from the Apollo Bunder and was well known to seafaring men. It was closed daily at sun-set. It was demolished between the years 1862 and 1865.

(*b*) HODGE'S RAVELIN, 1862.

(*c*) THE SOUTH-WEST RAVELIN, BOMBAY, 1862.

A reference to the map of Bombay drawn in the year 1863 will show the positions of these two projecting portions of the fortifications.

No. 38. (*a*) THE RAMPARTS AND LOOK-OUT TOWER, BOMBAY CASTLE.

(*b*) PART OF THE BOMBAY FORT, THE OLD BRAB TREE.

(*From a photograph presented by the late Dr. Sydney Smith.*)

This appears to have been taken in the first decade of the 19th Century.

(*c*) The CHURCH GATE WITH THE WALLS IN COURSE OF DEMOLITION IN 1862.

(*See note to No.* 33 (*a*).)

No. 39. (*a*) BOMBAY, WITH ESPLANADE BANDSTAND.

(*b*) BOMBAY, VIEW OF CHURCH GATE, ESPLANADE.

These two views of Bombay were taken from prints in the collection of the late *Sir L. H. Bayley*, sometime Judge of H. M.'s High Court of Bombay, by permission of *Mr. Vernon F. Bayley*.

No. 40. VIEW OF THE ARSENAL.

The Arsenal which formed part of the Bombay Castle, came into the hands of the English in the year 1666, and was for nearly a century known as the Pattern Room. The Original building has, since 1888, been known as the Armoury.

No. 41. ELPHINSTONE CIRCLE, NORTH SIDE.

No. 42. ELPHINSTONE CIRCLE, SOUTH SIDE.

(*See also No.* 25 (*c*).)

The idea of replanning and utilising the Old Bombay Green as the site of business premises originated with Mr. Charles Forjet. The scheme was sanctioned by Sir George Clerk, Acting Governor from 1860 to 1862 and was completed during Sir B. Frere's term of office. The entire site of the old Bombay Green was purchased by the Municipality and resold in plots, which were mostly taken up by English mercantile firms, who gradually transformed the open space into an imposing example of street architecture. The suggestion to name the circle after Lord Elphinstone emanated from the representatives of the firms concerned in the construction of the different buildings, and was accepted at a meeting held in 1862. The work of building the circle was carried out under the supervision of Mr. James Scott.

No. 43. VIEW OF THE TOWN HALL, 1880.

No. 44. PARSEE BAZAR STREET.

From Elphinstone Circle to Gunbow Street. It was occupied by Parsee shop-keepers.

No. 45. APOLLO STREET.

From Elphinstone Circle to Colaba Causeway. It was widened soon after 1868.

No. 46. VIEW FROM WATSON'S HOTEL, 1880.

No. 47. THE SHIPPING FROM THE CUSTOM HOUSE.

No. 48. (*a*) THE TEMPLE OF MAHALUXMI, 1850.

(*See note to No.* 114 (*c*), *Places of Worship in Bombay.*)

(*b*) FORT OF BOMBAY FROM "BELMONT."

"Belmont" was a house situated on the declivity of Mazagon Hill.

(*c*) MALABAR POINT.

(*d*) "VAUCLUSE."

"Vaucluse" was a handsome English residence, placed in the midst of a cocoanut plantation on a point at the Breach opposite the Temple of Mahaluxmi.

View of Bombay. Taken from Mazagon Hill.

(*e*) SEWRI—THE NEAT'S TONGUE, BOMBAY.

Neat's Tongue was upon the Island of Trombay. The above sketches appear to have been made before the year 1850.

No. 49. SCENE AT THE CUSTOM HOUSE, 1880.

No. 50. PANORAMIC VIEW OF BOMBAY FROM MALABAR HILL.

This view was made about the year 1857 or shortly after, by the Rev. H. Carpendale.

The name "Malabar Hill" formerly included what is now called "Cumballa Hill." Its earliest notice is by Fryer in the year 1673. The name is derived from the Malabar pilgrims, who visited it in great numbers to bathe in the sacred tank. It is interesting to note that the hill attracted the attention of the early geographers and in a map which was drawn about the year 1583, we find it named "Cape Bombaim." Its oldest name is "Walkeshwar." To create a picture of the hill in olden times, we must blot out all the existing bungalows and carriage roads, leaving only one foot path which is now known as the "Siri Road." It was fairly well wooded, small game and monkeys being found in considerable numbers, Sir E. Nepean (Governor, 1812 to 1819) had a small cottage at Malabar Point, but for many years the hill retained its wild character, and it was not until the last half of the nineteenth century, that it became a residential quarter.

No. 51. VIEW OF BOMBAY TAKEN FROM MAZAGON HILL.

Mazagon Hill is an eminence on the Eastern side of the Island lying about two miles north of the Fort. From it a view can be obtained of the Fort, the City, the Harbour, the numerous islands, and part of the neighbouring mainland. It was, for this reason, considered one of the most beautiful spots in Bombay. The print is dedicated, by permission, to the Right Honorable Lord Viscount Falkland, G.C.B., Governor of Bombay, 1848-1853, by William Fallon, 1852.

No. 52. BOMBAY.

No. 53. (*a*) BOMBAY MAIDAN, 1850.

(*b*) BOMBAY SUPREME COURT ON LEFT, CUSTOM HOUSE AND DOCKYARD.

(*See note to No.* 39.)

No. 54. (*a*) LAKDI BUNDER, CHOWPATI, 1864.

This was situated near the turning of the road towards Walkeshwar, where the Port Trust Chowki now stands. This bunder was closed about the end of the last century. (Compare View of Back Bay, 1860, see No. 58 (*c*).)

(*b*) OLD ADMIRALTY HOUSE AND THE RECORDER'S COURT.

This building was the official residence of the Governor during the time of the Hon'ble W. Hornby, 1771-1784. It was, for its time, a palatial building. About the year 1786, a portion was used as the Town Hall, and in the year 1800, the Recorder's Court was also accommodated within it, a small portion being still retained as Admiralty House. About the year 1879, the Recorder's Court, which had been converted into the High Court, was removed to the modern building facing the Oval, and the Old Admiralty House was converted into the Great Western Hotel.

(*c*) SITE OF THE P. W. D., SECRETARIAT AND THE GENERAL POST OFFICE, 1864.

(*See note on No.* 33 (*a*).)

No. 55. MAPLA POR.

(*a*) FRONT VIEW.

(*b*) PLAN.

(*c*) SIDE VIEW.

In the year 1671, Gerald Aungier decided that " a fair common house wherein might be appointed chambers for the court of justice, warehouses and granaries for corn and ammunition, and prisons for several offenders " should be built. The Court of Directors, however, restricted the plan of the building to the construction of a Court House only, and accordingly orders were given in the year 1671 to commence the work. The building was completed in 1676. Here the Court House remained till the year 1720. The remains of this building are still to be seen on the west side of Bora Bazar Street, about 300 yards north of the north-west corner of the Elphinstone Circle, and constitute the oldest relic of British dominion in Bombay. It has received its name of Mapla Por from it being afterwards used as an enclosure for the property of "Maplas," a tribe of Arab Muhammadans from the Malabar coast, who during the eighteenth century controlled the bulk of coasting trade of Bombay. The original building suffered greatly from fire in the years 1803 and 1868, necessitating many alterations and additions to its former shape and structure.

No. 56. (*a*) View of Esplanade and outer Church Gate, 1864.

(*b*) View of Parel, 1864.

(*c*) View of Northern part of Bombay.

These pictures show the beginning of modern Bombay which dates from the year 1860.

No. 57. (*a*) View of Bombay from Salsette.

This view was painted by J. Wimber and shows the position of Sion Fort. The Fort is on the top of a small conical hill. It commands the passage from Bombay to the neighbouring island of Salsette and was of importance while the Marathas possessed that island. It was an out-post of British dominion in Western India for about a hundred years.

(*b*) Bombay Ice House.

The Ice House was built by public subscription in the year 1843, at a cost of Rs. 10,000. It was used for storing ice which was then being brought from America, the first consignment of ice being received in the year 1844. It was pulled down in 1917, having long fallen into disuse.

(*c*) Babula Tank.

Like most eastern cities, Bombay formerly possessed many tanks and wells, the water of which was used by the inhabitants of the City. A good example was the Babula Tank constructed in the year 1849. It was closed in the year 1907 by the Bombay Municipality. It was in close proximity to the Sir J. J. Hospital. The Tank was called after the "Babul tree" (acacia arabica).

No. 58. (*a*) A VIEW OF MAZAGON.

(*The House on the bluff is probably the "Mark House" by which ships were navigated.*)

The House on Mazagon Hill better known as "Mark House" was, in the early eighteenth century, kept white-washed to serve as a mark for vessels sailing up and down the harbour. There is a reference to this house in a letter of the Bombay Government to the Court of Directors in the year 1758.

(*b*) THE CASTLE, MALABAR HILL.

This is a photograph of an engraving made in 1893.

(*c*) VIEW OF BACK BAY, 1860.

The following account of the state of the foreshore of Back Bay, written about the year 1860, gives some idea of its insanitary state: "To ride home to Malabar Hill is to encounter sights and odours too horrible to describe, to leap over the mouths of sewers, to meet with impediments as one nears Chowpaty caused by boats and nets and stacks of firewood and to be choked by fumes from the open burning ghauts."

No. 59. (*a*) VIEW OF SEWRI, 1880.

The name "Sewri" is derived according to Dr. Gerson da Cuna, from "Sivadi", a little fort of Siva, the remains of which are still visible. In early times Sewri was a fishing village, surrounded by rice fields and salt pans. About the middle of the last century, the botanical garden of the Agri-Horticultural Society was located in Sewri, but it was subsequently transferred to Byculla, as the plot of land in question was required for a burial ground for the Christian community.

(*b*) VIEW OF BOMBAY FROM MAZAGON, 1834.

This view of Bombay Harbour made about 1834 formed one of the illustrations to the "Oriental Annual" by Caunter, of 1836. It appears to have been taken from an elevated position in Mazagon. Prior to the occupation of the Island by the Portuguese, this portion of the harbour was used as a landing place by the pilgrims from Malabar. Under the Portuguese, Mazagon attained some importance by being raised to the position of a Casaba (district), and there was built a Church and a religious house belonging to the Franciscans. Under the British, Mazagon was mainly occupied by cultivators, but after 1830, it began to attract the attention of the wealthy, especially of the English merchant class in Bombay, as a desirable site for residence, and many fine bungalows were erected in the vicinity. The hill on the right is Nowroji Hill, and the Colaba Light House may be seen in the distance.

(c) BACK BAY FROM MALABAR HILL, 1851.

The view from Malabar Hill, looking eastward across Back Bay, and the Harbour is one of the most attractive features of the City, and has been the theme of much descriptive eloquence.

No. 60. JUNCTION OF MEDOWS STREET WITH RAMPART ROW.

MEDOWS STREET is named after General Sir William Medows, who was Governor of Bombay and Commander-in-Chief, Bombay, 1788-1790.

RAMPART ROW WEST was formerly called Rope Walk Street "so called from the Rope Walk established by the East India Company for the manufacture of coir ropes."

No. 61. (a) FORT, NORTH, HORNBY ROAD.

This portion of the Town represents the area in which the Parsees and the other communities first began to settle about the year 1675, and its antiquity is proved by the existence of the remains of Aungier's original Court House and a Parsee Agiary of great age (in the picture to be seen opposite the Banyan tree). The photograph appears to have been taken shortly before or about the year 1872, as the tramway lines which were laid between the years 1872 and 1877 are not shown.

(b) FORT, SOUTH, RAMPART ROW.

This portion of the Fort lies on the east of Hornby Road. The photograph seems to have been taken at the same time as (a).

The central object of interest in the two is the Floral Fountain erected in honour of Sir Bartle Frere. The carriages called "Buggies" which have now entirely disappeared are to be seen in this photograph.

No. 62. FLORAL FOUNTAIN (TAKEN ABOUT 1880).

The fountain which now stands opposite Church Gate Street was intended by the Agri-Horticultural Society to be erected in the centre of Victoria Garden. The original cost was estimated at £2700. but the commercial crash of 1865, delayed the scheme. When it was revived it was found that the cost would be nearly £9,000. As the Agri-Horticultural Society had then ceased to exist, the whole scheme was modified and at the suggestion of Mr. Arthur Crawford, it was decided to erect the present fountain made of less costly materials than had been originally intended, upon the site it now occupies. It is raised in honour of Sir Bartle Frere to commemorate his progressive policy in the administration of Bombay. In the year 1908, a large portion of the grass plot which surrounded the fountain, was removed to provide more room for pedestrian and horse traffic.

No. 63. OLD MUNICIPAL OFFICE.

Was located in a house lying between Watson's Hotel and the Sassoon Mechanics' Institute from 1870 to 1893. This was pulled down and the site is now occupied by the Army and Navy Co-operative Stores.

No 64. (*a*) WARDEN ROAD.

From Nepean Sea Road to Tardeo Road. It was named after Francie Warden, a prominent Bombay Civilian.

(*See Note No.* 129.)

(*b*) THE ORIENTAL BANK.

A good representative of the style of building of the year 1851, when the Oriental Bank was first established in Bombay.

No. 65. VIEW OF THE HARBOUR FROM THE BALL TOWER.

Time is communicated to the Harbour by ball signal from Bombay Castle every week day at 2 P.M., throughout the year.

No. 66. (*a*) MALABAR HILL FROM ST. XAVIER'S, BOMBAY.

The St. Xavier's College (now High School) is a plain but most capacious building on the Esplanade Cross Road. It was built by the Roman Catholic Clergy of this Presidency. This building was commenced in the year 1868 and completed in 1873, at a cost of Rs. 2,62,194, towards which sum Government contributed over Rs. 61,000, the balance being made up by the subscriptions of the Catholic Clergy and Laity.

(*b*) Bombay City from Malabar Hill.

The portion of the City, which is seen covered with thick cocoanut plantations, has recently been laid out by the City Improvement Trust.

No. 67. (*a*) Government House, Parel.

The House, originally a convent belonging to the Jesuits, was confiscated from the Society in the year 1689, by Government on account of their political intrigues against the British. Its healthy situation and pleasant environment caused it to be used as the occasional residence of the Governors of Bombay up to the year 1829. It was then made the permanent residence of the Governor of Bombay and was occupied as such until 1883. Mr. Grose, who visited the house in 1750, found it "to be a pleasant mansion house with a fine garden." W. Hornby, Governor of Bombay, used it as an occasional residence in 1776. About 1803 Sir James Mackintosh, then Recorder of Bombay, occupied rooms in it, and described it as "being a noble building with magnificent apartments and two delightful rooms for his library." The building was again occupied as Government House and enlarged and embellished by the Hon'ble Mountstuart Elphinstone (1819-27) and further repaired and refurnished during the Governorship of Viscount Falkland, Sir Seymour Fitzgerald and Sir P. Wodehouse. Owing to a variety of causes it ceased to be occupied during the Governorships of Lord Reay and Lord Harris, when the small bungalow at Malabar Point was gradually enlarged and transformed into a permanent residence for the Governor. It was then offered to the Municipal Commissioner for the use of the Victoria Jubilee Technical Institute, but was not considered suitable. In the year 1897, upon the outbreak of the plague, it was used as a plague hospital, and in 1899 the Plague Research Laboratory occupied a portion of the building. Additions and structural alterations have since been made, and a fine range of Laboratories have been erected. Thus this building, which in past times was the scene of many brilliant entertainments and receptions, is now one of the chief centres in India of medical research, and affords accommodation to a School of Tropical Medicine.

(*b*) APOLLO BUNDER, BOMBAY.

The building in the centre was occupied as a restaurant started by one Mr. Green. This building was removed in consequence of the changes made at the Bundar.

No. 68. (*a*) VIEW FROM THE OFFICE OF THE "BOMBAY GAZETTE."

The "Bombay Gazette" after being for many years one of the two representative morning papers in Bombay, has ceased to exist.

(*b*) VIEW FROM THE ESPLANADE HOTEL.

Showing the crescent as it was before the Prince of Wales Museum of Western India was erected.

No. 69. (*a*) BHENDY BAZAR.

Part of the Parel Road from Pydhowni to Grant Road is known as Bhendy Bazar from a row of Bhendi trees north of Pydhowni. The Jain Temple belongs to the Swetambari Jains and is stated to contain large quantities of jewellery and precious stones.

(*b*) MARKET ROAD, BOMBAY.

This portion of the town was pulled down recently by the City Improvement Trust, and rebuilt.

No. 70. (*a*) OLD SECRETARIAT.

In the year 1757 Government purchased this house from Mr. J. Spencer and transformed it into a Government House. In this house, Governor Jonathan Duncan died in the year 1811, after which it was discarded in favour of the Government House at Parel. In the year 1829, it was used for the offices of the Secretariat and continued to be so occupied till 1883. It was sold by Government in 1886. There are many references to it in the writings of early travellers.

(*b*) Mazagon Castle, Side view.

(*c*) Mazagon Castle, Front view.

Mazagon Castle, the residence of the family of Sir Jamsetji Jijibhoy, Bart., was the scene of several entertainments held in honour of distinguished persons, who visited Bombay from the year 1824. Lord Elphinstone, Lord and Lady Falkland, H. R. H. The Prince of Wales (afterwards H. M. King Edward VII), Sir Richard Temple, Lords Ripon and Dufferin and others were entertained here.

No. 71. Hydraulic Lift at Hog Island.

This lift was designed to serve as a dry dock for vessels belonging to Government, particularly for troopships. Its cost was about £350,000. When it was finished, by the contractors, Sir Philip Wodehouse, Governor of Bombay, invited a large number of guests to witness the opening ceremony. The party set sail from Bombay in a large vessel upon which the great power of the lift was to be illustrated, but the demonstration did not take place. The hydraulic machinery was very powerful and was calculated to lift with ease a vessel of 25,000 tons but the scheme was a failure. About the year 1886, the P. & O. Company purchased and repaired the lift, but a weight of more than 7,000 tons was never risked upon it. It ceased to be used in a few years and was dismantled. A bundor, with the four bare walls of the power house and two or three disintegrating caissons are all that now remain of the venture.

No. 72. (*a*) The City from St. Xavier's.

The picture affords a view of Esplanade Cross Road. The Church seen in the photograph is the "Free Church of Scotland" opened for Divine Service on the 29th of October 1848. It was built by means of subscriptions raised chiefly through the exertions of Dr. Wilson and Rev. A. Garden Fraser. This

Church was sold in the last decade of the last century, when the present church facing the Maidan in Waudby Road was built.

(*b*) THE COTTON GREEN, BOMBAY.

The present Cotton Green is situated at Colaba, and was first set apart for storing cotton in the year 1844. It comprises an area of one and a half square miles. Each dealer rents a plot according to his requirements. Bombay, after New Orleans is the greatest cotton port in the world. Business generally commences after midday. It is now under contemplation to remove the Cotton Green from Colaba to Mazagon.

No. 73. THE GREAT BANYAN TREE.

This is an engraving of a painting made in the year 1805 by James Wales from a drawing made on the spot by James Forbes in the year 1778. It is dedicated "To William Hornby and the Gentlemen of the Bombay Club." Mr. Forbes calls it "View of Cubeer Burr," the celebrated Banyan tree, which stood on the bank of the Narmada. The following extract is taken from Forbes' "Memoirs." "The Banyan tree is called by the Hindus "Cubeer Burr" in memory of a favourite saint, and the one I am describing, is much resorted to by many English gentlemen from Broach. Its circumference is nearly two thousand feet measured round the principal stems and the overhanging branches cover a much larger space. This pavilion affords a shelter to all travellers, and one of the English chiefs of the times used to encamp under it in magnificent style." This tree was supposed, during Forbes' time, to be the same as described by Nearchus.

No. 74. (*a*) PYDHOWNI POLICE STATION.

This marks the site where in former times people from Worli used to wash their feet, after crossing the deep channel which separated that Suburb from the native City.

(*b*) OLD MUNICIPAL OFFICE, APOLLO STREET.

In this building, which now contains the office of the Society for the Prevention of Cruelty to Animals, was located the Municipal Office about the year 1868.

No. 75. (*a*) The Old timber stacks at Mazagon.

These lands were reclaimed in the the year 1904-1905.

(*b*) View of Back Bay, from an old painting, about 1870.

(*c*) Malabar Hill, taken from near the spot where the Iron Duke's bungalow stood.

(*See Note to No.* 77.)

No. 76. (*a*) Reclamation work at Chaupati, 1864.

These reclamations were made in 1864. Chaupati is really Chaupati (four channels) and is evidence of the inroads of the tides through the breach before the Western foreshore was reclaimed.

(*b*) A view from Malabar Hill.

(*c*) Chaupati, an Estate recently developed by the Improvement Trust.

No. 77. Walkeshwar Road.

This portion is now non-existent, but was formerly that part of Malabar Hill on the right hand as one ascends the Siri Road, and was described by a writer in year 1856 as situated between the Ridge Road and the sea. This brow of the hill was cut away in the year 1865 to provide fillings for the Chaupati reclamation.

No. 78. Victoria Gardens, 1880.

About the year 1830, the Agri-Horticultural Society of Western India was founded to establish a botanical garden. The cost of the upkeep of this garden was met by subscriptions of members, donations, and an annual grant from Government. A large plot of land was granted by Government, near Sewri, and during the first years of its existence considerable activity was displayed by the Society. The ground at Sewri was resumed by Government in 1862, but meanwhile Mr. (The late Sir) George Birdwood had converted into a garden and pleasure ground, some orchards and lands on the Mount Estate. This ground was taken over by the Agri-Horticultural Society and was named the Victoria Gardens. The grounds were laid out in an artistic manner and were opened to the Public by Lady Frere in 1862. When the Agri-Horticultural Society ceased to exist the gardens were taken over by Government and were further improved. Zoological specimens were added at a later date. In consequence of certain financial adjustments between the Municipality and the Government, the cost of the upkeep of the Gardens and their management was handed over to the former body. It now comprises an area of about 50 acres. It contains a good collection of the flora of tropical climes; but the chief attraction for visitors consists in its zoological collection. Great improvements in the housing and exhibition of the animals took place between the years 1900 and 1905 at the instance of Mr. W. L. Harvey, I.C.S. the Municipal Commissioner.

No. 79. Hornby Vellard.

This vellard was built between Love Grove Hill and Breach Candy to stop the inroad of the sea which formerly swept over a large tract of land now comprised within the area between Byculla Flats, and Pydhowni. William Hornby, who was Governor of Bombay from 1771 to 1784, perceived that the first steps towards improving the sanitary condition of Bombay was to shut out the sea at Breach Candy and for this purpose appealed to the Court of Directors for a grant of a lac of rupees to construct the vellard. The permission was not given, but disregarding this, at the approach of the close of his term of office Governor Hornby commenced the work and had it completed within eighteen months. His action was censured by his superiors, but has been praised by posterity. The great result of his foresight and energy was that it rendered available for cultivation and settlement the wide area of low-lying ground in the centre of the Island and welded its eastern and western shores into one united area.

No. 80. Robert Money School. Dhobi Talao.

The establishment of this school was due to the efforts of early English missionary workers in the field of education in the City. It was built by a Member of the Church Missionary

Society in the year 1857 in memory of Robert Money, Secretary to Government, Educational Department. It stood on the edge of the Esplanade till the year 1909 when the property was sold and a new school built in Procter Road.

The fountain in front of the school premises, was erected in honour of Sir Seymour Fitzgerald, in the year 1867. It was removed and re-erected on the northern boundary of the Maidan.

No. 81. Bohra Bazar Street.

(From Fort Street to Gunbow Street).

This is one of the oldest thoroughfares in the Fort retaining its original lines. When the traveller Parsons visited Bombay in 1755, he wrote "The Streets within the Fort are well laid out and the buildings (namely gentlemen's houses) so numerous and handsome as to make it an elegant town" This part of the town suffered much from the destructive fire of 1803 which destroyed nearly three-fourths of the Bazar. It was quickly rebuilt, without any marked alterations in the alignment of the street.

No. 82. Cursetjee Maneckji Statue.

This statue commemorates the memory of Cursetji Maneckji Shroff, who lived about the year 1830. He was an army contractor and supplied the Duke of Wellington's army with rice in the year 1803, and was subsequently involved in long litigation over the contract in the courts here and in England. The statue was erected on the top of a column in Bellasis Road by his son Maneckji Cursetji, who distinguished himself later on as a prominent citizen and a Judge of the Small Causes Court.

No. 83. Mahaluxmi Temple.

No. 84. Fishing Boats in the monsoon in the northern part of Bombay Harbour.

Governors of Bombay.

No. 85. (1) SIR GEORGE OXENDEN. 1619-1669.

Sir George Oxenden's family is said to have derived its name from Oxendon in the Parish of Nonington, Kent, and to have resided in that county since the reign of Edward III. On 18th September 1662, Sir George Oxenden was appointed President and Chief Director of all the East India Company's affairs "at Surat and other Factories in the East as far as the Red Sea". In the year 1668 when the Royal Charter, by which His Majesty King Charles II bestowed Bombay upon the H. E. I. Company, was granted, Sir George was appointed the first Governor under the Company's rule. He resided only for a short time in Bombay, dying at Surat on July 14th, 1669, where he was buried. As Governor of Bombay he framed a set of regulations for its administration and inaugurated the policy of suppressing the Maratha pirates on the Western Coast of India. He conceived the idea of building a Church for the English in the Island but did not live to see his idea carried out.

(2) CHARLES CROMMELIN.

Charles Crommelin was the son of Marc Antonine Crommelin of a Hugenot family. He joined the East India Company's service in Bombay, 1732, and was Governor of Bombay from 1760 to 1767. He returned to England, suffered losses in trade and again settled in India in 1772, as a free merchant. He was residing at Canton in 1777, and accepted the post of British Consul at Goa in 1784, where Mr. J. Forbes mentions having met him. The date of his death is unknown.

(3) JONATHAN DUNCAN. 1756-1811.

Jonathan Duncan arrived in Calcutta in the East India Company's service in 1772, and was Governor of Bombay for the unprecedented period of 16 years, from December 27th of 1795

Sir. Geo. Oxenden, 1668.

Hon. Mountstuart Elphinstone, 1819.

to August of 1811. He died in the Old Secretariat building at Bombay, and was buried in St. Thomas' Cathedral, where a monument was erected in his honour. Upon this is the following inscription : "He was a good man and a just. He abolished infanticide in Benares and Kathyawad".

Photograph of a Mezzotint by W. Waid after a portrait painted in 1792 by Masquerier.

(4) THE HON'BLE MOUNTSTUART ELPHINSTONE. 1779-1859.

Mountstuart Elphinstone was the fourth son of Lord Elphinstone and was born on October 6th of 1779. He was educated at the High School, Edinburgh. In the year 1795, he came to Bengal as a writer in East India Company's service, was placed in diplomatic service under Sir Barry Close at Poona in 1801. He served with Sir Arthur Wellesley in 1803, and as Commissioner in Berar 1804. From 1808-1810 he was with the Embassy to Kabul, and from 1810-1817, he was Resident at the Court of Poona. From 1817 to 1819 he was Commissioner administering the conquered Mahratta provinces and from 1819 to 1827, he was Governor of Bombay. After his retirement he spent some time in travelling, but mostly in retirement in England where he died on November 28th of 1859. His Government of Bombay was nearly faultless. His efforts for the education of Indians were untiring, and are commemorated in the Elphinstone High School and the Elphinstone College in Bombay. In every other department of Government his influence for good was seen and his name will remain as that of a great, just, and a true Governor. A statue to his memory is to be seen in the Town Hall, and a bust by Noble was erected in the year 1860 in the Victoria and Albert Museum by Members of the Elphinstone College.

(5) JOHN FITZGIBBON; THE EARL OF CLARE. 1792-1851.

Lord Clare was born on June 20th, 1792. He was the son of the first Earl, who was Lord Chancellor of Ireland, and succeeded his father in 1802. He was educated at Christ Church

College, Oxford, and held the Governorship of Bombay from 1831 to 1835, being the first Governor appointed under a new Act "For the better government of His Majesty's Indian Territories". He died on August 18th of 1851.

No. 86. (1) SIR ROBERT GRANT. 1779-1838.

Sir Robert Grant was the second son of Charles Grant and was born in Bengal in 1779. He was sent to England in 1790, and was educated at Magdalene College, Cambridge. He was called to the Bar at Lincoln's Inn in 1807, and was elected a Member of Parliament for various constituencies from 1818 to 1834. He advocated Jewish Emancipation from civil disabilities. He was Judge Advocate General in 1832, was Knighted in 1834, and appointed Governor of Bombay in 1835. During the term of his short administration many useful works were carried out. Colaba was joined to Bombay by a causeway and a portion of land was reclaimed upon which the buildings now known as Grant's Buildings were erected in the year 1838. The Bombay Chamber of Commerce was established in 1836. The condition of Love Grove was improved by making sluices and main drains, and the great road now called the Grant Road was constructed. In the year 1838, Sir Robert Grant supported the syndicate which had been formed to start the "Bombay Times." He died at Dapoli, near Poona, on July 9th, 1838, and was buried at St. Mary's Church, Poona. He was the author of a "Sketch of the History of the East India Company from its first foundation to 1773," and other works, and some sacred poems several of which, have been printed in Palmer's "Book of Praise." The Grant Medical College was founded in 1845 in memory of Sir Robert Grant, a moiety of the cost of the building being defrayed by Sir R. Grant's friends, and the rest by Government.

(2) SIR JAMES RIVETT CARNAC, BART. 1785-1846.

Sir James Rivett Carnac was the son of Mr. James Rivett, a Member of the Bombay Council, who on the death of his brother-in-law, General Carnac, added to his own, the name of Carnac. He entered the R. M. A. Woolwich in 1800 and joined the East India Company's Madras Native Infantry in 1801, but was shortly afterwards transferred to Bombay. He was A. D. C. to the Governor, Jonathan Duncan, and served against the Marathas in 1802, retiring from the army as Major in 1822. Upon his return to England he was appointed a Director of the East India Company in 1827, was made Chairman in 1830 and returned to India as Governor of Bombay in 1839, an appointment he only held for two years. He died on January 28th, 1846. A scholarship named after him was founded in his honour and his bust was placed in the Town Hall.

(3) Sir George Arthur, Bart. 1784-1854.

Sir George Arthur entered the army in 1804, and served in Italy, 1806, and in Egypt, 1807. He was Military Secretary to the Governor of Jersey, and Lieutenant-Governor of British Honduras from 1814 to 1822. He was Lieutenant-Governor of Upper Canada from 1837 to 1841, and Governor of Bombay from 1842 to 1846. After retirement, he was made a Privy Councillor. He died on September 19th, 1854.

(4) John; Lord Elphinstone, G.C.B. 1807-1860.

Lord Elphinstone was the son of John, 12th Lord Elphinstone, and was born on June 23rd, 1807. He entered the Royal Horse Guards in 1826, and was Lord-in-Waiting from 1835 to 1837. He was Governor of Madras from 1837 to 1842. While in Madras, he encouraged the practice of resorting to the Nilgris during the hot weather. He travelled in Kashmere and Upper India and returned to England in 1845. He was appointed Governor of Bombay in 1853 and held the appointment till 1860. During the time of the mutiny, he showed his capacity for administration, and it was largely due to his efforts that the rising did not spread to Bombay. He rendered further service to the Government of India by sending troops from Bombay to the disaffected parts of the country. During his administration, great improvements in Bombay were inaugurated, and many reforms were introduced in the Municipal Administration of the City. The Vehar Water Works were commenced, a scheme for the drainage of the City was prepared, and the work of reclamation was begun. Lord Elphinstone supported Sir (then Dr.) George Birdwood to establish a Government Central Museum of Economic Products and Industry in the year 1855, which, upon its completion some years afterwards became the Victoria and Albert Museum. He was raised to the Peerage of the United Kingdom in 1859 and he died on July 19th of 1860. A statue was erected in his honour by the public of Bombay in 1860, and was placed in the Town Hall. The present Elphinstone Circle is named after him.

(5) Sir Bartle Frere, K.C.B., G.C.B. 1815-1884.

Sir Bartle Frere was born on March 29th, 1815, and received his education at Bath and Haileybury. He showed his individuality of character from an early period of his career, for he came out to India in 1834 by an unusual route, *via* Cairo, Jeddah and Mocha and from thence in a pilgrim vessel to Bombay. He was appointed Assistant Revenue Commissioner for some years in investigating land assessments, was Private Secretary toSir G. Arthur, Governor of Bombay, 1842, was Resident at Satara, 1846, and after its annexation was appointed its Chief Commissioner. He was Chief Commissioner in Sindh from 1850 to 1859. His great services in Sindh as Commissioner were rewarded with K.C.B. in 1859. He was a Member of the Governor-General's Supreme Council from 1859 to 1862, when he was appointed Governor of Bombay. The creation of the modern City of Bombay must be always associated with his name; for besides bringing to completion the works begun by Grant and Elphinstone, he advanced education, built colleges, forwarded the construction of railways, demolished the old fortifications of the City, reclaimed portions of land on the western and eastern foreshores, and projected and commenced those great buildings and architectural ornaments which have been the pride of the City. He retired in 1867, and was a Member of the Secretary of State's Council of India from 1867 to 1877. He was President of the Geographical and Asiatic Societies and accompanied H. R. H. the Prince of Wales

Sir Bartle Frere, 1862.

(H. M. the late King Edward VII) on his Indian Tour, 1875-1876. In 1877 he was appointed Governor and High Commissioner in South Africa, where he was engaged in the wars with the Kaffirs and the Zulus in 1878-1879, and was recalled in 1880. He died on May 29th of 1884, and was buried in St. Paul's Cathedral. In Bombay, the Floral Fountain was erected opposite Church Gate Street in his honour, and his statue by Woolner was placed in the Town Hall, and a bust was placed in the University Building.

No. 87. (1) SIR SEYMOUR FITZGERALD, K.C.S.I., G.C.S.I. 1818-1885.

Sir Seymour Fitzgerald was born in 1818. He received his education at Oriel College, Oxford, and was called to the Bar at Lincoln's Inn in 1839. He was Member of Parliament for Horsham from 1852 to 1865, and Under Secretary for Foreign Affairs from 1858 to 1859. He was appointed Governor of Bombay in 1867, and retired in 1872. He again entered Parliament, 1874, but only remained one year. He died on June 28th, 1885. The "Fitzgerald Fountain and Lamp" now placed at the northern end of the Maidan was erected in his honour in 1867.

(2) SIR PHILIP E. WODEHOUSE, K.C.B., G.C.S.I. 1811-1887.

Sir Philip Wodehouse was born on February 26th, 1811. He entered the Ceylon Civil Service in 1828, and after occupying high appointments in British Honduras, British Guiana, and in South Africa, was appointed Governor of Bombay in 1872 and held this post till 1877. He died on October 25th, 1887.

(3) SIR RICHARD TEMPLE, BART. 1826 to 1902.

Sir Richard Temple was born on March 8th, 1826. He received his education at Rugby, and Haileybury. He arrived in India in January 1847. Shortly afterwards being appointed to the post of Secretary to the Punjab Government. In 1860, he was made Chief Assistant to the Financial Council. In 1862, he was made Chief Commissioner of the Central Provinces, and was Resident at Hyderabad in 1867, Foreign Secretary to the Government of India in 1868, Financial Member of Council from 1868 to 1874, in which year he was appointed by Lord Northbrook to superintend the famine operations in Bengal. He was made Lieutenant Governor of Bengal in 1874 and appointed Governor of Bombay in 1877, retiring in 1880. He greatly assisted in the movements of troops to Malta and Afghanistan during the Russian and Afghan troubles of 1878-79.

After his retirement he entered Parliament in which he was a conspicuous figure. He died on March 15th, 1902. His statue by Brock was erected in Bombay by public subscription.

(4) SIR JAMES FERGUSSON, BART., G.C.S.I., K.C.M.G., C.I.E., LL.D. 1832.

Sir James Fergusson was born in 1832 and was educated at Rugby and University College, Oxford. He entered the Grenadier Guards in 1851, and served in the Crimean War, being wounded at Inkerman. He retired from the army in 1856. He was Under Secretary for the Home Department, 1867-68, Governor of South Australia, 1868, of New Zealand, 1873-1875 and was Governor of Bombay from 1880 to 1885. During Sir James' administration the history of Bombay was characterised by much activity in Municipal Administration, by the further growth of the Island Trade, and by large public benefactions.

(5) DONALD J. MACKAY; LORD REAY. G.C.I.E., G.C.S.I., LL.D. 1839.

Lord Reay was born in 1839 and was educated at Leydon University. He was Member of the Second Chamber of the States General, Netherlands, 1871 to 1875, and was naturalised in England by an Act of Parliament in 1877, was made a Peer of the United Kingdom in 1881, Rector of St. Andrews in 1884, and was Governor of Bombay from 1885 to 1890. It was during the time of his administration that the great Jubilee celebrations of 1887 were held in Bombay. A statue in bronze by Alfred Gilbert was erected in his honour on the northern end of the Oval. Lord Reay took a keen interest in all educational matters, especially in Technical Education. The foundation of the Victoria Jubilee Technical Institute and the Reay Art Workshops at the Sir J. J. School of Art commemorate his efforts towards the advancement of Indian Craftsmanship.

No. 88. (1) GEORGE ROBERT CANNING LORD HARRIS, G.C.S.I., G.C.I.E., D.L. 1851.

Lord Harris was born on February 3rd, 1851. He was educated at Eton and Christ Church, Oxford. He was Under Secretary for India, 1885 to 1886, Under-Secretary for War, 1888 to 1889, and was appointed Governor of Bombay in 1890. He was a well-known cricketer, playing for Kent and England, and it was due in a great measure to his encouragement that cricket and other forms of outdoor sport were taken up by Indians of all classes in Bombay. During Lord Harris' term of office, the City was convulsed by an outbreak of very serious Hindu and Muhammadan rioting on the 11th August 1893. The rioting continued for three days when through the intervention of the military, quiet was gradually restored. Lord Harris served in South Africa in 1901 and is still living.

(2) WILLIAM MANSFIELD ; LORD SANDHURST, G.C.I.E., G.C.S.I. 1855.

Lord Sandhurst was born on August 21st, 1855, and is the son of the first Baron Sandhurst. He was educated at Rugby. He entered the army in 1873, but retired shortly after. He was Under Secretary for War, 1886, and again from 1892 to 1894. He was appointed Governor of Bombay in 1895. In the year 1896, the City was visited by plague, which first appeared in a Chawl near the Musjid Bridge, and spreading thence, wrought the greatest havoc among the population. As one of the means to stamp it out, Lord Sandhurst founded in the year 1898 the City Improvement Trust. He retired in 1899.

(3) HENRY STAFFORD ; LORD NORTHCOTE, G.C.B., C.I.E. 1846-1907.

Lord Northcote was born on 18th November 1846, and was the second son of Sir Stafford Northcote, afterwards Earl of Iddesleigh. He was educated at Eton and Merton College,

Oxford. He was Private Secretary to Lord Salisbury during his Embassy to Constantinople, 1876-1877, Financial Secretary to the War Office, 1885-1886. Surveyor General of the Ordinance, 1886-1887, Charity Commissioner, 1891-1892, Member of Parliament for Exeter, 1880-1899. He was appointed Governor of Bombay in 1899, when he displayed great energy in combating the ravages of plague in the City and famine in Guzerat. It was due to his foresight that the celebrated breed of Guzerat cattle was preserved during the latter visitation. He retired in 1903 to assume the post of Governor-General of Australia. He died in England in 1907.

(4) Charles W. A. N. Cochrane Baillie; Lord Lamington. 1860.

Lord Lamington was born on July 29th, 1860. He was educated at Eton and Christ Church College, Oxford. He was Member of Parliament for North St. Pancras, from 1886 to 1890, Governor of Queensland, 1895 to 1901, and was appointed Governor of Bombay in 1903. The most notable event during his term of office was the visit to India of T. R. H. The Prince and Princess of Wales. Lord Lamington retired in 1907.

(5) Lord Sydenham. 1848.

Sir George Sydenham Clarke, son of the Rev. W. J. Clarke of Knoyle House, Folkstone, was born on 4th July 1848. He was educated at Wimbledon School and Haileybury. He was the first of his year to pass into and out of the R. M. Academy. He entered R. E. in the year 1868. He was on the staff of the R. I. E. College, Cooper's Hill from 1871 to 1880. He saw service in the Egyptian Expedition, 1882, Sudan Expedition, 1885. He was employed at the War Office till 1892, and was Secretary to the Colonial Defence Committee from 1885 to 1892, Secretary to the Royal Commission on Navy and Army Administration, Member of the Committee on War Office Reorganisation from 1900 to 1901, Governor of Victoria (Australia), 1901-1904, Member of the War Office Reconstitution Committee, 1904, Secretary to the Committee of Imperial Defence, 1904-1907 and Governor of Bombay from 1907 to 1913.

During his term of office T. Ms. The King Emperor and Queen Empress landed in Bombay on the 2nd December 1911, *en route* to Delhi where the Imperial Durbar to announce their Coronation was held on the 12th of that month. He was raised to the Peerage in 1913. Lord Sydenham took great interest in schemes for the development and improvement of the City of Bombay, and large irrigation projects were started in the Presidency during his governorship. He gave considerable attention to educational problems, especially to the adequate teaching of Science and Economics. The Institute of Science and the Sydenham College of Commerce and Economics are the practical outcome of his interest in these subjects.

No. 89. Richard Bourchier. 1689-1770.

Richard Bourchier applied to the Directors of the East India Company for permission to reside at Madras as a Free Merchant in 1718, and seems to have gone to Madras and settled there, and was engaged in what was termed "The Country Trade." In 1725, he was appointed as Chief of Anjengoon on the Malabar Coast. In 1749, he was transferred to Bombay, as second in Council and in the following year, he succeeded Mr. Wake as Governor and President at Bombay, and held the office for a period of little more than nine years. The chief event during his terms of office was the capture of Gheria from Angria by Clive. He died in 1770.

No. 90. Major-General William Medows. 1738-1813.

William Medows was born in 1738 and entered the army as Ensign in 1756. From 1760 to 1764 he served in Germany and subsequently as a Lieutenant-Colonel in the American War, when he distinguished himself at the battle of Brandywine, where he was wounded. He came to Madras in 1782, and defeated a French Fleet off Tricomallee. He then returned to England. He was Governor of Bombay from 1788 to 1790. He was then transferred to Madras as Governor and Commander-in-Chief and he immediately opened the campaign against Tipoo Sultan. He returned to Madras in 1792 and received addresses from the people. He was created C.B. and sailed for England during the course of the year. He died in 1813.

No. 91. Sir Evan Nepean, Bart. 1751-1822.

Sir E. Nepean, son of Nicholas Nepean, was born in the year 1751. He entered the Navy as a clerk. He was Under Secretary of State in the Shelburne Ministry. In 1794, he was Under Secretary for the War; from 1795 to 1804 he was Secretary of the Admiralty. He was created a Baronet in 1802. He was Chief Secretary for Ireland in 1804, and was appointed Governor of Bombay in the year 1812. He held the appointment for seven years; he died on October 2nd, 1822.

The photograph was taken from the original painting by Gainsborough and was presented to the Museum by Sir Charles Nepean, Bart., of Appleshaw.

No. 92. Sir George Russel Clerk, K.C.S.I., G.C.S.I. 1800-1889.

Sir George Clerk, son of John Clerk, was educated at Haileybury. He entered service as a Writer to the H. E. I. Co. in 1817, and after holding some minor appointments in Bengal, he entered the Political Department. He served in Rajputana, at Delhi, Umballa, Lahore and other places. He was Lieutenant-Governor of the North-West Provinces in the year 1843, and in the following year was Provisional Member of the Supreme Council. He was appointed Governor of Bombay in the year 1847, which post he vacated in the following year, and again held the same office for two years from 1860. On his return to England he was successively Under Secretary and Secretary to the Board of Control from 1856 to 1858 and Permanent Under Secretary of State for India from 1858 to 1860. He was Member of the Secretary of State's Council from 1863 to 1876. He was made K.C.S.I. in 1861 and G.C.S.I. in 1866. He died on 25th of July 1889.

This photograph of a pencil sketch by Lord Colville, of the late Sir George R. Clerk, G.S.C.I., K.C.B., was presented by his grandson, Sir George Russel Clerk, K.C.M.G., C.B.

Photographs of Improvement Schemes, undertaken by the City of *Bombay Improvement Trust*:—

No. 93. View of Undria Street Scheme.

No. 94. View of Undria Street Scheme.

No. 95. View of Sion-Matunga Scheme.

No. 96. View of Sion-Matunga Scheme.

No. 97. Quarrying Work at Nowrojee Hill.

No. 98. View of Sandhurst Road, East.

No. 99. View of Chunam Kiln Street.

No. 100. (*a*) View of Hughes Road.

(*b*) View of Sandhurst Road.

(*c*) View of Old Mathew Road.

No. 101. View of East Agripada.

No. 102. View from Sandhurst Road to Crawford Market.

No. 103. View of Sandhurst Road, East.

No. 104. View of Dadar Scheme, showing Kingsway.

No. 105. View of Parel Scheme.

No. 106. View from Queen's Road to Carnac Road.

These prints from No. 93 to No. 106 were taken from negatives, kindly lent by the Chairman of the City Improvement Trust.

Places of Worship in Bombay.

No. 107. (*a*) St. Thomas Church from an old print.

(*b*) St. Thomas Cathedral, about 1860.

St. Thomas Cathedral is the oldest Anglican Church in Bombay. Before 1675, the English in Bombay had no Church of their own, the only place of divine worship being a room set apart in the Castle and called the Fort Chapel. Sir George Oxenden entertained the idea of providing a proper Church and the Governors who immediately succeeded him supported the scheme. A subscription list was started which resulted in the collection of Rs. 50,000 mostly from amongst the servants of the Company. The present site, then a portion of the Bombay Green was selected, and by the year 1681 the walls of the building had been erected. For some reason the work was stopped; it has been said the stoppage was due to misappropriation of the funds, but certain it is that nothing further was done till the year 1714 when the Rev. Richard Cobb came to Bombay. At his earnest entreaty, a second subscription list was started, headed by the then Governor the Hon'ble W. Aislabie, and the work of completing the building was taken in hand. It was opened for service on the Christmas Day of the year 1718 during the Governorship of Mr. Charles Boone. The nave of the present Church is the original structure, but the tower as it stands was not built till 1839, and the chancel was added in 1863. Further improvements were carried out in the year 1906. The fountain at the entrance is the gift of Sir Cawasji Jehangir.

The Church contains in its muniment chest two ancient silver chalices. One of these was presented by Gerald Aungier in the year 1675, and the other bears the following inscription: "The gift of the Greenland merchants of the city of York in

1632." The organ is a very fine one, built by Bishop and Starr at a cost of Rs. 15,000.

(*c*) St. Andrew's Church.

This Church is situated at the corner of Apollo Street. The Scots in Bombay first held Divine Service in the Mess Room of the Town Barracks near the Shipping Office, and then in a room in the Old High Court, but their increasing number enabled them to build a Church in the year 1818. A site was obtained from the Court of Directors of the East India Company and the building was completed in the year 1826. The steeple was struck by lightning soon after its completion, but was rebuilt in the following year.

No. 108. (*a*) The Pottinger Memorial Church, Colaba.

Erected to the memory of Major E. Pottinger (1811-1843) who came to Bombay in the Artillery 1827. He became assistant to his uncle Sir H. Pottinger, Resident at Sindh, and was sent in 1837 to explore Central Asia. He arrived at Kabul, disguised as a horse-dealer and reached Herat. Here he assisted the Afghans, when Herat was besieged by the Shah of Persia in 1837-1838. He was appointed Political Agent at Herat. He served in the Afghan campaign of 1842, and went to China in 1843, where he died in Hongkong.

(*b*) The Old Muniment Chest in St. Thomas' Cathedral.

In this are preserved the two silver chalices of considerable age mentioned under No. 107 (*a*).

(*c*) Governor J. Duncan Memorial.

See note on J. Duncan, Governor of Bombay, 1795-1811, *No.* 85 (3).

No. 109. (*a*) Katherine Kirkpatric Memorial.

(*b*) Memorial to Thomas Carr, First Bishop of Bombay.

In the year 1835, Bombay was raised to the dignity of a Bishopric, when Dr. Carr was appointed its first Bishop. He was installed on the 21st of February 1838, and held the post till 1851 when he resigned on account of ill-health.

(c) MEMORIAL TO CAPT. G. N. HARDINGE, R.N.

He was a younger brother of Lord Hardinge, Governor-General of India, 1844-1848.

No. 110. TEMPLE OF MUMBADEVI.

The worship of this Goddess has been prevalent in Bombay from an early date, and the first temple in her honour appears to have been built by the early Koli inhabitants of the Island. It was situated near the Phansi Talao on a spot now included within the limits of the Victoria Terminus Railway Station. About the year 1737, this temple appears to have been removed by order of Government, and a new one was erected on the present site on the Parel Road by one Pandu Sonar about the year 1753. There is in front of it a large tank, which is referred to in her Journal by Mrs. Graham, who visited the temple in the year, 1832.

(b) TEMPLE OF WALKESHWAR.

The worship of Siva in the form of a Lingam under the title of Walkeshwar, dates from the time of the Silharas in the Island of Bombay. The Silharas ruled about the 9th century of the Christian era. The original temple is believed to have been destroyed by either the Muhammadans or the Portuguese. The present temple was built about the year 1715 by Rama Kamat and the management at present is vested in a Board of Trustees appointed by the members of the Goud Saraswat community. Formerly the temple derived a large measure of sanctity from its proximity to a cleft rock at the very end of Malabar Point and known as Sri Gundi (Lucky Stone).

No. 111. (a) MAHIM CREEK AND OLD PORTUGUESE CHURCH.

This Church is one of the oldest monuments of the Portuguese rule in the island of Bombay. It was built in the sixteenth century by the Franciscans and is dedicated to St. Michael. It continues to receive an annual grant from the British Government.

(*b*) ROMAN CATHOLIC CHURCH.

This Church which is situated at Bhuleshwar is said to have been built with the money obtained from Government for an old church, which, during the time of the Portuguese occupation of the island, was situated on the Esplanade not far from the Cross, which now stands on the maidan near the Native Infantry Lines. This Church was pulled down in the year 1760 by order of Government for strategic reasons.

(*c*) CHRIST CHURCH, BYCULLA.

This Church was built for the pupils of the Bombay Education Society's School, on a portion of the old artillery grounds at Byculla in the year 1833, the Society contributing a sum of Rs. 10,000 towards its cost. The foundation stone was laid by Lord Clare.

No. 112. THE JUMA MOSQUE.

This Mosque was first situated near Dongri Fort and was built by Konkani Muhammadans. It was removed during the administration of Mr. Bourchier (1750-1760) and a new mosque was erected on the Esplanade. This was also pulled down in the year 1770 and the present building was built on a site in Shaik Memon Street. The building was commenced in the year 1775 and completed in the year 1802. It was erected over a tank by one Nathu Patel, Headman of the Muhammadan butchers in Bombay. It was subsequently enlarged and repaired in the year 1837 by the late Mr. Muhamad Ali Rogay. The management of the building and the property attached is vested in a Board of Directors elected by the Konkani Muhammadans, while the executive functions are delegated to a Nazir, appointed by the Board. The annual income of the Mosque is about Rs. 75,000.

No. 113. THE DURGAH AT MAHIM.

This shrine is erected in honour of a Muhammadan saint "Pir Makhdum Fakih Ali Saheb" and is the only interesting architectural monument of the time when Bombay was under Muhammadan Rule. The Pir, according to the writing of Syid Gulam Muhamad Rufai, one of the Trustees of the Mahim

Durgah in his biography of the Saint. was born in the year 776 A. H. or 1372 of the Christian era, and was a profound scholar of Arabic literature and Islamic theology. He is said to have written more than one hundred books, the chief among these being a commentary on the sacred Al Koran. He died in the year 1431 A. D., when the shrine was built over his remains. The original building was repaired about the year 1674 and again in the year 1748. A fair is annually held in honour of the Pir and is generally known as the Mahim Fair.

No. 114. (*a*) Temple of Bhuleshwar.

The Temple of Bhuleshwar is dedicated to the worship of Siva. It is situated in the busiest portion of the city in the district of the same name. The accounts of its origin differ. The first temple is said to have been built about two hundred years ago, but there is no record to show that this is correct, or to indicate why and when it was demolished. The present temple was built about the year 1830 at a cost of Rs. 40,000, raised by subscription, and at present its management is vested in a Board of Trustees appointed by the Goud Saraswat community. The temple is built of black stone and the interior is decorated with ornamental work of an elaborate character.

(*b*) Temple of Babulnath.

The original temple of Babulnath was built about the year 1780, and is situated on the south-east slope of Malabar Hill. It is dedicated to the worship of Siva. The present temple with all its costly carving was completed about the year 1900, and its management rests in the hands of Vanias and Bhatias in the City.

(*c*) Temple of Mahaluxmi.

This temple is situated at Breach Candy and contains the images of Mahaluxmi, Mahakali, and Maha Saraswati. The worship of these three Goddesses dates from very early times and it is recorded that the original Kolis and Agrees patronis ed a temple here. According to a legend the building of the present temple is ascribed to one Ramji Shewji, a contractor, who found the images buried in the sea, at the time when the work of constructing the Hornby Vellard was in progress. Ramji obtained the land from Government on which the temple now stands.

Streets and Houses.

No. 115. A STREET IN BOMBAY, 1867.

A distinctive feature of street architecture in Old Bombay was the elaborate carving of the wooden pillars, beams, and the brackets of the houses. The wood-carving of Bombay was celebrated and this illustration affords a characteristic example of its style. The rich effect obtained by carving was in many instances enhanced by colour; red and green being the favourite colours. This reproduction is from a water colour sketch taken by W. Simpson in 1867.

No. 116. BOMBAY GIRLS' SCHOOL.

(*Drawn by W. Simpson in* 1867.)

The modern movement in favour of the education of women is one of the results of the spread of Western ideas throughout India. Miss Mary Carpenter, who came to India in the middle of the last century writes: "a number of young men who had been educated at the Elphinstone College, have formed themselves into a body called 'The Students' Society' for the purpose of educating the female portion of the population. They taught the girls themselves in schools supported at their own expense, and in course of time they employed Pandits in default of native female teachers."

This drawing shows one of the early schools for girls in Bombay.

No. 117. THE BYCULLA CLUB.

The movement to found this Club arose from the sentiment responsible for the existence of the "Sans Souci" Club founded in 1785 and of the Highland Society in 1821. These clubs possessed no property or permanent premises and neither had a lengthy existence. In 1832, a meeting to promote the foundation of a club with permanent premises was held, and after considerable difficulty and delay had been experienced in the choice of a suitable site for the building, it was thought advisable to rent a property in Mazagon, known as the "Grove." The proposal fell through, but a club was established in the Byculla Assembly Room under the title of the Byculla Club in the year 1833. The Assembly Room formed a portion of the Race Stand attached to the old Race Course, which was then known as the Byculla Turf. This room is now the Club Reading Room. Additions to the building were made from time to time up to the year 1906. Among the noteworthy features at present are the extensive gardens which contain rare and valuable plants. As the oldest club in Bombay and one of the oldest in India, it has always held a foremost place in the social life of the European community of the City. During the last eighty years, its members have entertained a great number of distinguished visitors and officials. The earliest entertainment of this character is believed to have been a dinner held in honour of Chevalier Venturas, General of the army of Ranjit Singh. Members of the Royal Family have been entertained. H. M. The King Emperor and H. M. Queen Mary when they visited India in 1905 as Prince and Princess of Wales, H. R. H. The Duke of Connaught, and H. R. H. the late Prince Albert Victor having honoured the Club by their presence. For many years Viceroys and Governors have been entertained at dinner on the eve of retirement, and this opportunity has been utilised to make many interesting and important pronouncements by the chief guest.

No. 118. (*a*) NAKHODA TANK.

This tank was built on the Esplanade between St. Xavier's College and Elphinstone High School in the year 1856 by Nakhoda Muhamad Ali Rogay, at a cost of about Rs. 50,000.

(*b*) HEAD OFFICE OF THE BOMBAY VOLUNTEER RIFLES.

This building is situated on the Esplanade Cross Road and was formerly used as a Sailor's Home before the permanent building was erected at the Apollo Bunder. It is a typical example of the earlier style of domestic architecture in Bombay.

No. 119. (*a*) DHOBI TALAO AND THE FRAMJI CAWASJI INSTITUTE CONTAINING THE BOMBAY NATIVE GENERAL LIBRARY.

This tank gave its name to a busy locality, but the tank has now been filled in. It was also called the Framji Cawasji Tank by order of Government to commemorate the liberality of that citizen in spending a large sum of money on its reconstruction in the year 1839.

There was no public library in Bombay during the 18th century. The Hon'ble East India Company had a small library for the use of its officers and men. A meeting was held in a house near Trinity Chapel, Dhobi Talao, when a proposal was made to establish a library for the use of the public. At first the number of members of this library was seventy. When the Framji Cawasji Hall was opened, it was arranged to incorporate the Native General Library with it. In the year 1865, the hall was completed and the library was removed there.

(*b*) SITE OF THE OLD BHATIA BAUG

(*South of Victoria Terminus*).

This was so called because all along its south side, the Bhatia population greatly predominated, when the "Baug" so-called was first built in the latter part of the sixties.

The statue erected in honour of Dr. Thomas Blaney, C.I.E., 1823-1903, and now moved from the Bhatia Baug to the northern edge of the Maidan, commemorates the services he rendered to Bombay during a period of nearly half a century.

No. 120. WALKESHWAR.

"This little village is called Walkeshwar. In the middle of a large square is a tank round which are built temples, houses and tall white obelisk-shaped pillars, called Deepmals, painted in parts red and green on which lamps are suspended on great festivals, and a number of little altars containing the Tulsi Plant. Temples of all sizes and shapes are here; there is the lofty one shaped like a sugar loaf—here one with a domed roof, on it a pinnacle and turret, with similar ones at each corner, and another elaborately carved, in which are small images of gods in niches placed in the numerous turrets on the roof."—*Chow-Chow* by Viscountess Falkland.

No. 121. (*a*) APOLLO BUNDER, 1857.

This interesting picture is reproduced from a photograph taken at the time of the Mutiny.

(*b*) APOLLO BUNDER.

No. 122. PANORAMIC VIEW OF BOMBAY TAKEN FROM MALABAR HILL.

No. 123. PANORAMA OF PART OF THE COTTON GREEN AT COLABA, SHOWING THE ARRANGEMENT OF THE COTTON BALES IN JATHAS.

(*See Note No.* 72 '*b*'.)

Portraits of the Kings and Queens of England connected with the History of the Island of Bombay.

No. 124. KING CHARLES II. 1630-1685.

Born on 29th May 1630. Married Catherine of Braganza on May 22nd, 1662. Died February 6th, 1685, and was buried on February 14th in Westminster Abbey.

No. 125. QUEEN CATHERINE. 1638-1705.

She was the daughter of the Duke of Braganza, who in the year 1640 became John IV of Portugal. The marriage of King Charles with Queen Catherine was brought about chiefly through the services of Fr. Domingos, an Irish priest, who was Confessor to the Queen Regent of Portugal. When at the Court of France, Fr. Domingos had already met with and known intimately King Charles II, who was then in exile. Upon Charles being restored to the throne of England, Domingos proposed to the Queen Regent of Portugal a matrimonial and political alliance with England, a proposal cordially approved by the Queen. Accordingly the treaty of marriage was drawn up on the 23rd of June 1661, between the King of England Charles II, and the Infanta of Portugal, Donna Catherine. It was ratified on the 28th of August 1661 by the Queen Regent on behalf of her son the King of Portugal, Don Alfonso VI. By this treaty the Crown of Portugal ceded and granted to the Crown of England, the Island and harbour of Bombay in full sovereignty as part of the dower of Donna Catherine. The treaty was bitterly opposed by the Portuguese authorities in India, who placed every obstacle possible in the way of its provisions being carried out, but despite this opposition, Bombay Fort and Island were eventually handed over to the British Crown.

No. 126. HIS MAJESTY KING EDWARD VII, 1841-1910.

H. M. King Edward VII, King of the United Kingdom of Great Britain and Ireland, and of all the British Dominions beyond the seas, Emperor of India, was the eldest son of H. M. Queen Victoria, and was born at Buckingham Palace on the 9th of November 1841. He received his education at Christ Church College, Oxford, and Trinity College, Cambridge. In 1858, he was made a Knight of the Garter, and received a commission as Colonel in the army, ascending in due time to the rank of a Field Marshal. In 1859, he travelled in Italy and Spain and in the following year he visited the United States of America and Canada. In 1862, he went to Palestine accompanied by Dean Stanley, whence he returned after four months' travel. He was married on the 10th of March 1862 to Princess Alexandra (born, 1st December 1844), daughter of Christian IX, King of Denmark. The marriage ceremony took place in St. George's Chapel, Windsor. His visit to India in the year 1875 was a political event of great importance. He left England on the 11th of October and landed in Bombay on the 8th of the following month. He was received at the Bundar by the Viceroy, Lord Northbrook, and while in Bombay, received a large number of Indian Feudatory Princes, whose acquaintance he subsequently improved by visiting their courts during the seventeen weeks he spent in the country. On the 22nd of January 1901 he succeeded his mother H. M. Queen Victoria and was crowned on the 9th of August 1902. A grand Durbar of the Indian Chiefs and People was held in honour of this auspicious occasion at Delhi on the 1st of January 1903 by His Excellency Lord Curzon. He died on the 6th of May 1910. The late King Edward manifested a keen interest in all questions affecting the welfare of his people in every portion of the British Empire, and he was specially solicitous in his support of every movement designed to ameliorate the hardships of the poor. During the life time of his mother, he, as Prince of Wales, bore much of the burden of court ceremonials and public functions. He was a fine sportsman, and a first class shot. He was one of the most far-seeing and accurate judges of foreign affairs, and during his short reign was recognised throughout Europe as one of the greatest diplomatists of the age. By his frequent visits to continental capitals, he did much to allay international animosities and promote peace and good will, and it was due mainly to his tact and influence, that the " Entente " between England and France was brought about.

No. 127. Her Majesty Queen Alexandra.

(*See note to No.* 126.)

Portraits of Civilians.

No. 128. (*a*) SIR FRANK SOUTER, 1831-1888.

Little is known of Sir F. Souter's life before he served as a Volunteer against the rebels in the Nizam's dominions, in 1850. He was appointed Superintendent of Police at Dharwar, in 1854. In the time of the Mutiny he captured the Nurgoond Maratha Chief, for which he received a sword of honour, and he suppressed the Bhil brigands in North Deccan in 1859. He was appointed Commissioner of Police in Bombay in 1864, and held the appointment till 1888. He was made C.S.I. in 1868, was knighted by H. R. H. The Prince of Wales at Bombay in 1875, and was made a C.I.E. in 1886. He was a Member of the Bombay Municipal Corporation from 1872 till his death, which took place in the Nilgris on June 5th, 1888. A memorial in the form of a bust was raised in his honour and placed in the garden of the Central Police Office, Bombay.

(*b*) MR. CHARLES FORJETT, 1810-1890.

Of the early life of Mr. Forjett little is known, prior to his appointment firstly as Deputy, and later as Commissioner of Police, Bombay, in 1855. During his term of office, he was also the Municipal Commissioner of the City. Shortly after the outbreak of the Mutiny in 1857, he discovered a plot among the sepoy regiments in Bombay to rise and murder their officers, and the energetic action he then took, prevented an outbreak. The plot was hatched in the house of one Ganga Prasad in Sonapur and it was intended that two risings should take place on nights during the Muharrum and Diwali holidays. Mr. Forjett frustrated the plot by arresting Gunga Prasad, and succeeded in bringing the guilty parties to justice. He was rewarded for this, was presented with purses, and received an extra pension on his retirement. He died on January 27th, 1890.

No. 129. Francis Warden, Esq.

(*Engraved by William Walker from a picture by J. Harges in* 1851).

Francis Warden was a distinguished Bombay Civilian, who came to India in the year 1769. In 1818, he was Chief Secretary to the Bombay Government and was one of the prominent members of the "Sans Souci" Club, the first club formed by Englishmen in the City. He was a Member of the Bombay Council in the year 1819, but seems to have given up the appointment in the latter part of the year. He was re-appointed to the Bombay Council in 1823, and occupied the post till 1826, when he finally left India. He is the author of "A Report on the Landed Tenures in India" written about the year 1814 and is credited as being the first man to whom we are indebted for bringing Aungier's Convention of 1672 before the public.

No. 130. (*a*) Right Rev. Louis George Mylne, D.D., 1843.

The Right Rev. L. G. Mylne, son of Major Charles David Mylne of the East India Company's service, was born on 20th April 1843. He received his education at Merchiston Castle School, Edinburgh, St. Andrew's University and Corpus Christi College, Oxford. He was Assistant Curate of North Moreton, Berks, from 1867 to 1870, Tutor at Keble College, Oxford, from 1870 to 1876, in which year the degree of Doctor of Divinity was conferred upon him. He was appointed Bishop of Bombay in 1876, an appointment which he held till 1897. Upon his return to England he was appointed Vicar of Woodford and Wilsford and Canon of Salisbury Cathedral and retained this office till 1905, when he was appointed Rector of Alvechurch. He is the author of "Sermons preached in Bombay" and various Charges and Sermons and wrote many articles in the "Church Quarterly Review," etc.

(*b*) Right Rev. Reginald Heber, 1783-1826.

Bishop Heber, son of Rev. Reginald Heber, was born on April 21st, 1783. He was educated at Whitchurch, and at

Brasenose College, Oxford. He was the author of "Carmen Saeculare", which he wrote in 1800, and gained the Prize for English Verse for his "Palestine" in the year 1803. Two years later, he won the English Essay Prize, and was appointed Fellow at All Soul's College, Oxford. He travelled for two years in Europe, and was ordained in the year 1807. He was appointed to the living of Hodnet in 1807, Prebendary of St. Asaph's in 1812, and was appointed Bishop of Calcutta in 1822. While in Calcutta, he completed the Bishop's College. He travelled extensively through the whole of India and Ceylon, and published an account of his travels in his famous book "Journey through India, from Calcutta to Bombay, with notes upon Ceylon and a Journey to Madras and the Southern Provinces". He died at Trichinopoly on 3rd of April 1826. He composed 57 hymns, which were published in the "Christian Observer." A statue is erected to his memory in St. Paul's Cathedral, Calcutta.

(c) RIGHT REV. HENRY ALEX. DOUGLAS, D.D., 1821-1875.

Bishop Douglas, son of Henry Alex. Douglas, was born on 22nd February 1821. He received his education at Glasgow University and Balliol College, Oxford. He was ordained after taking his degree in 1845, in which year he was appointed Dean of Cape Town. He was appointed Bishop of Bombay in the year 1868. He died in London on December 13th, 1875.

No. 131. SIR JAMES MACKINTOSH, M.P., 1765-1832.

(From an original picture by Sir T. Lawrence, R.A., in the possession of Josiah Wedgewood, Esq.)

Born on October 24th, 1765. He was educated at Fortrose, and Aberdeen University. He studied medicine at Edinborough, but relinquished this for the law. He was called to the Bar in 1795 and came to Bombay in May 1804. He visited Poona in 1805 and was presented to Baji Rao, the last Peshwa. He afterwards made a tour through the Deccan extending over a thousand miles. While in Bombay, from 1804 to 1808 he lived at Government House, Parel, which was placed at his disposal by Governor Duncan. Here he penned his brilliant correspondence with his friends in England. Afterwards he lived at "Tarala" (Palm Green) at Mazagon from which house, a magnificent view of the City and Harbour could then be obtained. On the death of the first Recorder of the Court of Bombay, Sir James was appointed to the post, which he held till 1811. His journals, written while in Bombay, are extremely instructive. He founded the Bombay Literary Society which grew later into the Bombay Branch of the Royal Asiatic Society, of which he was the first President. He left Bombay in 1811.

No. 132. CAPTAIN JOSEPH HUDDARD, F.R.S.

(*Engraved from the original picture in the possession of Charles Turner, Esq., by I. Blood*).

Capt. Huddard surveyed the Eastern Coast of India.

No. 133. SIR JOSIAH CHILD, 1630-1699.

Sir Josiah Child was the son of a London merchant. He made a large fortune as a Victualler to the Navy at Portsmouth, and became a Director, and eventually Chairman of the East India Company, in which, for the last twenty years of the 17th Century, he held a dominating position. He died in June 1699.

No. 134. (*a*) SIR GEORGE BIRDWOOD, 1832-1917.

Sir George Birdwood was born at Belgaum in December 1832 and received his education at Plymouth Grammar School, and Edinburgh University. He entered the Bombay Medical Service in 1852, and served in Persian War during 1856 to 1857. On his return to Bombay he took a prominent part in the life of the City, displaying special activity in raising endowments to the newly established University from the Indian Community. He was for some time Professor at the Grant Medical College, Curator of the Government Central Museum, and Honorary Secretary of the Bombay Branch of the Royal Asiatic Society. He was one of the founders, together with the late Dr. Bhau Daji, of the Victoria and Albert Museum, and designed and laid out the Victoria Gardens. He returned to England in 1876, to join the staff of the India

Office as Special Assistant in the Revenue and Statistical Department. He held a leading position in all the principal International Exhibitions from 1857 to 1901. He was given C.S.I. in 1877, created K.C.I.E., 1877, and the Honorary Degree of LL.D. (Cambridge) was conferred on him in 1886. He was the author of several books on the Industrial Products of India, on Indian Art and wrote many official reports upon economic, religious and archæological subjects connected with India. He died in 1917.

(*b*) REV. JOHN WILSON, D.D., 1804-1875.

John Wilson was born on December 11th, 1804. He was educated at Edinburgh University, were he studied Medicine. He was ordained Missionary of the Scottish Missionary Society in 1828. He arrived in Bombay in 1829 and was the first to establish schools for Indian girls, and a Church for Indian converts on Presbyterian principles. He closely studied the vernaculars and became Superintendent of the Free Church of Scotland's Indian Mission at Bombay. He travelled extensively in the Bombay Presidency collecting manuscripts and acquiring knowledge of oriental subjects. He was President of the Bombay Literary Society in 1835; Member of the Royal Asiatic Society, 1836; President of the Cave Temple Commission appointed to examine the antiquities connected with the Cave Temples, from 1848 to 1861; Vice-Chancellor of the Bombay University in 1868; and the Head Curator of the General Assembly of the Free Church of Scotland in 1870. He died on 1st December 1875 in Bombay and lies buried in the Queen's Road Cemetery. He was the author of "The Laws of the Bible," "Suppression of Infanticide in Western India," "Hindu Religion," "Caste among the Hindus," and "India three thousand years ago." The Wilson College, Chaupaty, Bombay, is a memorial of his work in the City and Presidency.

(*c*) JAMES FORBES, 1749-1819.

A member of the Bombay Civil Service, he came out to Bombay in the year 1765, and remained till 1783, serving in different places. During the seventeen years of his stay in India, he gathered together a large collection of sketches and notes on the fauna and flora of the places he visited, and was a keen observer of the religion and manners of the people. The materials thus collected, he utilised for his work "Oriental Memoirs" which he published in four large volumes between 1813-1815. After his return to England he lived in learned ease and retirement and died on August 1st, 1819.

Portraits of Military and Naval Officers.

No. 135. **Field Marshal Arthur, Duke of Wellington,** 1769-1852.

(*Painted by Sir W. Bechey, R.A., engraved by W. Skelton and published in* 1814.)

Arthur Wellesley was the fourth son of the first Earl of Mornington. He was educated at Chelsea, Eton, and subsequently at the Military College at Angers in France. He entered the army in 1787, and after passing through several regiments, became Major and Lieutenant-Colonel in the 33rd Regiment in 1793. In the year 1796, he was sent with his regiment to India, and was engaged in the war with Tippu of Mysore. Tippu's forces were routed by him and Seringapatam was closely besieged. On its capture and the death of Tippu, Wellesley was placed in command of Seringapatam and subsequently administered the province of Mysore as Governor. Two years later, he was appointed to take command of a body of troops collected for foreign service in Ceylon. He was then placed under General Baird, who was directed to lead his army against Napoleon in Egypt and it was at this time, about the year 1801, that Wellesley came to reside in Bombay. He lived in a house called "Surrey Cottage" which stood half way up the Eastern slope of Malabar Hill near Siri Road. The house comprised a somewhat spacious and lofty hall, with wings and long verandahs at the sides and back. It commanded a view of Back Bay, and a portion of Girgaum, also the Esplanade and the Fort. Wellesley was prevented from following the expedition to Egypt by an attack of fever, and was shortly after engaged in the war with the Marathas, when he gained his two great victories at Assaye and Argaum. He again visited Bombay about March 1803 and remained till the month of July 1804. His second visit was marked by his triumphal entry into the City on the 13th of March. The route by which he entered the City can still be traced. It stretched from the Dock Gate opposite the Old Court House to the Old Secretariat, then known as Government House. The course of the procession "was lined from end to end by all the troops then in the garrison and packed by a dense mass of human beings." In Bombay, he was presented with a sword of honour and before he left for England, was made a K. C. B. The remainder of his career is included in English and European History.

The Wellington Fountain in Bombay at the Southern end of Apollo Street, was erected as a memorial of his visit to the City.

No. 136. (*a*) Sir James Outram, Bart., 1803-1863.

Born on January 29th, 1803. He received his education at Aberdeen and entered the Indian army at the age of sixteen, first landing in Bombay as Acting Adjutant of a Bombay regiment in 1820. He was married in Bombay, and he was offered the command of the Poona horse. He was employed in Kandesh and succeeded in improving the condition of the Bhils. By founding his Bhil Corps, during the period of his appointment as Political Agent at Mahi Kantha in Gujrat from 1835 to 1838, he was able to reduce the turbulant chiefs of the province. In 1838 he was attached to the Staff of Sir John Keen, who commanded the Bombay Army which took part in the operations in South Afghanistan. In 1839, he was Political Agent at Hyderabad in Sind, and in 1841 in Upper Sind and cultivated the friendship of the Amirs. In 1842 while on a visit to Bombay he was entertained at a public dinner attended by about 150 citizens and presided over by Mr. Fawcett of Messrs. Remington & Co., when he was presented with a sword costing 300 guineas. He defended Hyderabad Residency in 1843, and was made Lieutenant-Colonel and C. B. He was Resident at Satara in 1845 and at Baroda in 1847, when he exposed corruption among officers occupying high posts. He was Resident at Lucknow in 1854 and later on in 1856, when Oudh was annexed was made its first Chief Commissioner, and a K. C. B. He was given the command of the Expeditionary Force sent against Persia in 1856 and at the conclusion of the war in 1857, was made a G. C. B. During the Indian Mutiny, he commanded two divisions of the Bengal army, and although senior officer attached to the relief column to Lucknow chivalrously refused to displace its Commander, Sir H. Havelock. He was Military Member of the Supreme Council from 1858 to 1860, when he retired. He was made a K. C. S. I. in 1861. He died on March 11th, 1863, and was buried in Westminster Abbey. Prior to his leaving India, he received from the Bombay Public a large silver shield. He was a keen sportsman, and he is said to have killed between the years 1825 and 1834, 191 tigers besides many other large animals. Sir Charles Napier described him as the "Bayard of India," and his exploits and his great character have made him conspicuous among the heroes of Indian history. Bombay possesses no memorial erected in his honour though he was closely associated with its history for a period of forty years.

(*b*) Major-General Sir Archibald Campbell, Bart., 1769-1843.

(*Engraved by J. Cochran. Painted by J. Wood.*)

Born, March 12th, 1769. He entered the army in 1787, and arrived in Bombay in 1788. He served under Sir R. Abercromby, 1790-1792, saw service in Mysore in 1792, at Cochin 1795, and was at the first seige of Seringapatam, 1799. He served in Portugal under Sir John Moore, 1808, and commanded a Portuguese regiment in 1810. He was knighted in 1814, made K. C. B. in 1815, returned to India with his regiment in 1821, and commanded the force in the First Burmese War of 1824-1826. He took Rangoon and Prome, and marching on Ava, concluded the Treaty of Yendabu in 1826. For these services he was made G. C. B. He returned to England in 1829, was made a Bart. and Lieutenant-General, 1838, but was unable through illness to accept the appointment of Commander-in-Chief, Bombay, in 1839, and died on October 6th, 1843.

No. 137. FIELD MARSHAL, LORD NAPIER OF MAGDALA AND CARYNGTON, 1810-1890.

Born in Ceylon on December 10th, 1810. He was educated at Addiscombe, and joining the Bengal Engineers at Calcutta in 1828, was employed on the Eastern Jumna Canal Irrigation Work in 1831. He returned to Europe to study Engineering and Railway work from 1836-1839. On his return to India, he laid out the hill station of Darjeeling and made the road thither and in 1842 laid out the Cantonment at Umballa. In the Sutlej Campaign of 1845 and 1846. He was severely wounded at Sobraon. He was promoted Major and commanded the force which took the hill fort of Kangra in 1846. He directed the siege of Multan in the Panjab Campaign of 1848 and became Civil Engineer to the Board of Panjab Administration in 1849, in which office he executed great public works, including roads, canals, buildings, bridges and frontier defences. He served in further expeditions in 1852 to 1853 and became Chief Engineer to the Commissioner of the Panjab in 1856 when he was promoted Lieutenant-Colonel. In 1857 he was made chief of the staff under Sir James Outram, was wounded at the second relief of Lucknow, and was made General and given the C. B. in 1858. He served as second in command to Sir H. Rose at Gwalior, defeated Tantya Topi, and suppressed the mutiny in Central India, for which he was made K. C. B. He commanded a division in China in 1860 and was promoted Major-General in 1861. He became Military Member of the Supreme Council from 1861 to 1865 during which period he acted as Viceroy and Governor-General of India for a short time. He was appointed Commander-in-Chief of the Bombay Army in 1865 and commanded the Abyssinian Expedition of 1867-1868. He was made a Peer, G. C. B. and G. C. S. I. and appointed Commander-in-Chief in India in 1870. After his retirement from India in 1876 he was made Governor of Gibralter, a post which he held till 1883. He was promoted Field Marshal in 1883, and dying on January 14th, 1890, was buried at St. Paul's Cathedral.

No. 138. Sir Charles Malcolm, 1782-1851.

Rear Admiral of the White.

Sir Charles Malcolm was a brother of Sir John Malcolm, who was Governor of Bombay from 1826 to 1830. He saw considerable service in the war of the French Revolution, and was present in his brother's (Admiral Sir P. Malcolm's) ship at the cutting out of the vessels at Manilla in 1798. He was knighted in 1826. He was appointed Superintendent of the Bombay Marine in the year 1827 and arrived in Bombay in 1828. He held this post for ten years. He was elected the first President of the Bombay Geographical Society when it was established in the year 1832. In the following year, he left India for the benefit of his health, but returned after a year's absence and finally left India in 1838. During his term of office, large maritime surveys were conducted in the Red Sea, the Gulf of Aden, and the Persian Gulf.

No. 139. Stringer Lawrence, 1697-1775.

Major-General and Commander-in-Chief in the East Indies.

(Painted by Sir Joshua Reynolds in 1761 *and Engraved by R. Houston.)*

Born, March 6th, 1697. He entered the army in 1727; served in Spain, Flanders, and the Highlands in 1745, and was sent out by the Court of Directors in 1747, as Major at the garrison at Fort St. George. He commanded the troops in 1748, and was taken prisoner by the French in his attack on Ariancopan near Pondicherry, but was released in 1749. In the same year, he took Devicotta and was appointed by the Directors to be Commander-in-Chief in the East Indies in 1752. He relieved Trichinopoly with the help of Clive, and after defeating the French, captured Seringapatam. In his operations against the French, he was generally victorious. He was superseded in the command, when the 39th Regiment, the first King's troops arrived in 1754. He commanded at the defence of Madras during its seige by Lally in 1758-1759 and returned to England in 1759. He came to India again in 1761 as Commander-in-Chief, Member of Council and Major-General, and retired, April 1766.

He died in London, January 10th, 1775. He was called the "Father of the Indian Army;" as the first regiment of Indian Sepoys was enrolled under his orders. A monument was erected in his honour in Westminster Abbey.

No. 140. (*a*) ADMIRAL SIR E. SLADE, K.C.I.E., M.V.O.
(*b*) ADMIRAL E. FREMANTLE.
(*c*) ADMIRAL RICHARD.

These officers respectively commanded the East India Squadron. The chief work of the squadron during the time of their command was the establishment of a naval blockade in the Persian Gulf for the purpose of suppressing the arms traffic. It had been ascertained that arms were being imported from Europe into Muscat, whence they were freely distributed among tribes dwelling on the sea coast of Persia. From here, they passed into the hands of the Afghans, who distributed them among the tribes dwelling on the North-Western Frontier of India. The acquisition of modern arms and ammunition transformed the military value of these tribes, and measures had to be taken for the prevention of their supply. In the year 1910, a vigorous naval blockade was instituted which resulted in the total stoppage of this traffic.

ADMIRAL SIR E. JOHN WARRE SLADE, K.C.I.E., K.C.V.O.

Admiral Sir E. Slade, son of Rev. George Slade, was born on 20th March 1859. He was educated at Eton. He entered the Navy in 1872, Lieutenant, 1879, Commander 1894, Captain 1899. He served in H. M. S. "Hecla" during the Egyptian War in 1882, and was appointed Commander-in-Chief of the East India Squadron in the year 1909, which office he held for three years.

ADMIRAL THE HON. SIR E. FREMANTLE, G.C.B., C.M.G., F.R.G.S., J.P.

Admiral Sir E. Fremantle, son of the 1st Baron Cottlesloe, was born on the 15th June 1836. He was educated at Cheam School, Surrey. He entered the Navy in 1849, Lieutenant 1857, Commander 1861, Captain 1867, Rear-Admiral 1885, Vice-Admiral 1890, and Admiral in 1896. He saw service in the

Burmese War 1852, New Zealand War 1864-1866, Ashanti War 1873-1874, where he was severely wounded. On this occasion he received thanks of both Houses of Parliament. He was Commander-in-Chief in the East Indies, 1889-1891 and in China from 1892 to 1895 and at Plymouth from 1896 to 1899. He wrote the Prize Essay on Naval Tactics for which he received a Gold Medal, from the Royal United Service Institution in 1880. He has also written the lives of Hawke and Boscawen and has been a prolific writer on naval subject for magazines.

No. 141. (*a*) Rear Admiral W. R. Kennedy. 1838.

Admiral Sir William Robert Kennedy, son of John Kennedy was born on the 4th March 1838. He was educated at Cheam. He entered the Navy in 1851, was made a Lieutenant in 1857 Commander in 1867, Captain 1874, Rear-Admiral in 1889, Vice-Admiral in 1896 and Admiral in 1901. He served in Crimea in 1855 and China in 1859.

He was Commander-in-Chief of the East Indies from 1892 to 1895. He has written books chiefly on Sport and Travel.

(*b*) Lieutenant T. E. Lewis, I.N.

Commanded No. 4 Detachment and two armed pinnaces sent from Dacca to Chittagong where the 34th Regiment of Bengal Native Infantry had mutinied in 1857. He succeeded in quelling the mutiny.

(*c*) Sir Charles Napier, 1782-1853.

Sir C. Napier was born on August 10th, 1872. After serving in Spain in 1808, in the United States in 1813, and against Napoleon in 1815, he held various military appointments in England until he landed in Bombay in 1841. He was in command of the army in Sind in 1842 and fought and won the battle of Meeane in 1843 against the armies of Sind and received submission of all the Sind Chiefs in 1844. He was made a G. C. B. in 1843. He defeated the hill tribes of the North West Frontier of Sind, 1844-1845. He was made a Lieutenant-General in 1846. He resigned the Government of Sind in the year 1847, but was Commander-in-Chief in India from 1849 to 1850. He suppressed a mutiny in an Indian Regiment and suspended on his own authority a government regulation on the subject of compensation allowance to the Indian Army. The Governor-General, Lord Dalhousie, expressing his disapprobation Napier resigned. He died on August 29th, 1853. A statue was erected in his honour in St. Paul's Cathedral.

No. 142. (*a*) COMMODORE FRUSHARD, I.N.

(*b*) OFFICERS OF H. M. S. "Severn".

(*c*) COMMODORE JAMES.

SIR W. JAMES, 1721-1793.

Born of poor parents Sir W. James went early to sea. He entered the service of the East India Company in 1747 and distinguished himself against Angria. He was made Commander of the Company's Marine Force in 1751, captured Sevendoorg, Angria's stronghold, in 1753, and Gheria in 1756 under Admiral Watson and Colonel Clive. He went to Bengal, taking with him the news of the declaration of war by the French and helped Clive to take Chandranagore in 1757. He returned to England in 1759. He joined the Board of Directors of the East India Company and was twice Deputy Chairman in the years 1778 and 1781. He was Chairman in the year 1789. He died on December 16th, 1793. His widow erected a tower on Shooter's Hill, near Blackheath, to his memory.

Burial Grounds in Bombay.

No. 143. (*a*) Christian Burial Ground, Queen's Road.

(*b*) Christian Burial Ground, Queen's Road.

(*c*) Burial Ground of the Daudi Bohoras, Queen's Road.

When the English settled in Bombay their first burial ground was at Mendham's Point, the space included in the area between the present Sailor's Home and Wodehouse Bridge. It was so named from one Mr. Mendham, who was the first Englishman buried there. In the year 1760, Government for strategic reasons closed the burial ground at Mendham's Point and opened a new cemetery at Sonapur (present Queen's Road) which was in use from 1763 to 1868. It was then closed and the present cemetery at Sewri was opened for burials. The cemetery has been walled in by a handsome iron railing.

No. 144. (*a*) Muhammadan Burial Ground, Queen's Road.

(*b*) Muhammadan Burial Ground, Queen's Road.

(*c*) Muhammadan Burial Ground, Queen's Road.

This is one of the oldest burial grounds in Bombay, having been in use from the time when the Muhammadans first settled in the Island.

No. 145. (*a*) Hindu Burning Ground at Walkeshwar.

(*b*) Burial Ground of the Lingayet Community

The Lingayets or followers of Basapa bury their dead as opposed to the mode of burning observed by all other high caste Hindus.

(*c*) Hindu Burning Ground, Walkeshwar.

The monuments seen in the picture are either tombs raised over the buried corpses of Sanyasis or Gosawees or "Chatrees"

(Umbrellas) raised to mark the particular spot where a distinguished individual was burnt.

No. 146. (*a*) HINDU BURNING GROUND, QUEEN'S ROAD.

(*b*) HINDU BURNING GROUND, QUEEN'S ROAD.

The Hindus in Bombay have occupied this site for the disposal of their dead from early times. Before the reclamation took place, it was situated upon the sea shore. Prior to the arrival of the English, they used this spot, for it is recorded that in the year 1677, when Gerald Aungier made his famous Convention with the Vanias of Surat, the privilege of using this site along with that of the other Hindus was extended to them. The present arrangements and increased facilities are due in a great measure to the efforts of the late Hon'ble Mr. Jaggonnath Shunkerseth.

No. 147. (*a*) PARSEE TOWER OF SILENCE.

A print taken from "Voyage from England to India" by Mr. Ives, published in 1754.

(*b*) PARSEE TOWER OF SILENCE.

A print taken from "Voyage to the East Indies" by Mr. Grose, published in 1772.

No. 148. PARSEE TOWER OF SILENCE.

A print made from a sketch taken about the year 1826.

No. 149. (*a*) PARSEE TOWER OF SILENCE.

(*b*) PARSEE TOWER OF SILENCE, 1915.

The Essex East Indiaman Refitted, and at Anchor in Bombay Harbour.

East Indiamen.

No. 150. THE "ESSEX" EAST INDIAMAN.

Captain John Strover.

In a heavy gale of wind, April 23rd, 1782, in which she lost her main and foremast, and was afterwards obliged to throw her guns overboard.

No. 151. THE "ESSEX" EAST INDIAMAN.

(*The morning after the storm showing her signal of distress to a ship in sight.*)

No. 152. THE "ESSEX" EAST INDIAMAN.

(*The afternoon of the same day, taken in tow by the "Byrangore" frigate and brought into Bombay.*)

No. 153. THE "ESSEX" EAST INDIAMAN.

(*Refitted and at anchor in Bombay Harbour.*)

These prints are inscribed to the Honourable East India Company. They represent the different situations of the "Essex" from the commencement of the gale to her safe arrival at Bombay.

No. 154. SKETCH OF THE "BALCARRAS."

(*East Indiaman, at North Fleet, Feb.* 1824.)

This was a fine ship built at Bombay, 1815, which was sold out of the H. E. I. Company's service in 1834. Her burden was 1,417 tons. She carried one hundred and thirty men and was armed with twenty-six 18-pounder guns. The vessel was finally sold for £10,000, and she sailed the sea for fifty years before being turned into a hulk.

No. 155. MARATHA GRABS AND GALLIVATS ATTACKING THE ENGLISH FLEET.

(From a picture in the possession of Mr. Rolinson.)

Sivaji had given a great impetus to Indian shipping and maritime enterprise, which led to the foundation of a formidable fleet. In 1698, Canoji Angria succeeded to the command of the Maratha Navy, and his career was one long series of naval exploits and achievements. Under him, the Maratha naval power reached its high water mark. Bombay had to fight with Angria for nearly half a century, before his power was subdued. In 1729, Canoji was succeeded by his son Sambhaji, who in turn was followed by Tukoji in 1743. In 1749, his fleets surrounded and cannonaded the "Restoration" of the Bombay marine. In 1754, the Dutch suffered a severe defeat by the loss of three large vessels one of which was loaded with ammunition. In the following years the English and the Peshwa jointly attacked his fleet. Severndoorg was reduced and this was followed by the expedition led by Admiral Watson and Clive against Gheria, resulting in the total destruction of Angria's fleet. The following is the description of Angria's fleet: "His fleet consists of grabs and gallivats. The 'grabs' have rarely more than two masts. They are very broad in proportion to their length. On the main deck under the forecastle are mounted two pieces of cannon, nine or twelve pounders, which point forward through the port holes cut in the bulk head, and fire over the prow; the cannon of the broad sides are from six to nine pounders. The 'gallivats' are large row boats rarely exceeding seven tons. They are covered with a spar deck made for lightness of slit bamboos, and these only carry pettera roes, which are fixed on swivels in the gunnel of the vessel, but those of the largest size have a fixed deck on which they mount six or eight pieces of cannon from two or four pounders. They have forty or fifty stout oars, and may be rowed four miles an hour."

No. 156. H. E. I. COMPANY'S SHIP "THOMAS COUTTS."

One of the later type of the H. E. I. Company's ships, having a chartered tonnage of between 1,325 to 1,350 tons. She was built by the East India Company on finer and cleaner lines than her predecessors in order to make a faster passage out and home; this particular vessel being noted for the following record :—

Commanded by Alex. Chrystie; left Blackwall for the East, March 12th, 1826; arrived at Bombay, June 2nd; sailed from Bombay to China on August 2nd; arrived at Singapore on August 26th; sailed from Singapore on the 28th; and arrived at Macao on September 11th. Sailed from China on November 23rd; passed through Java Head on December 10th; arrived at St. Helena on the 22nd of January 1827; left on the 24th and arrived at Downs on March 2nd, having made the quickest voyage out and home on record upto this date—10 days under one year.

This vessel was named after Thomas Coutts, a Scotch Banker, who died in 1822.

No. 157. H. M. S. "Asia."

The largest ship built in India before 1831 carrying 84 guns, and having a tonnage of 2,289. She was built for the British Navy in Bombay by Nowrojī Jamsetji Wadia, and floated out of the dock on 17th January 1824. She was fitted out for the Burmese expedition.

No. 158. (a) H. E. I. Company's Brig "Tigris."

The Brig "Tigris" was built in Bombay in the year 1829, its tonnage was about 258, and it carried ten guns.

On March 6th, 1836, the "Tigris" Commander, W. Igglesden, left Bombay for Torres Straits in order to inquire into the fate of the survivors of the barque "Charles Eton" which had been wrecked there. Under orders, the vessel was first to proceed to Sydney, but on account of stormy weather the vessel had to make for Hobart Town, which was reached on May 27th. On June 7th, the vessel sailed for Sydney. From Sydney she sailed for the Murray Islands, where she anchored on July 28th. From here the vessel proceeded to Half Way Island, and during the voyage she struck a patch of coral rocks north of Cape Croker and was saved from going to pieces on account of the strength of her timber. She lost her rudder, fore-foot, the whole of her false keel and twenty feet of her main keel. On the following day, she was steered into Raffles Bay by her head and after sails. Here the damage was repaired, and she proceeded on August 17th to Cowpang, and thence to Batavia and Bombay, where she arrived on November 7th, 1836. She was afterwards employed in the Euphrates Expedition, when she was lost in a hurricane on May 17th 1837.

(*b*) THE "BOMBAY" BURNT OF BUENOS AYRES.

(*c*). H. E. I. COMPANY'S STEAM FRIGATE "MEMNOS" 1,163 *tons.*

No. 159. (*a*) H. E. I. COMPANY'S FRIGATE "ELPHINSTONE."

The "Elphinstone" was built at Bombay in the year 1824, with a tonnage of 387 and carried 18 guns. She was in existence at the date of the abolition of the Indian Navy in 1863.

(*b*) AN OLD E. I. COMPANY'S MAN-OF-WAR A. D. 1670.

(*c*) THE "SEMIRAMIS."

The "Semiramis" was built at Bombay in 1842, with a tonnage of 1,031 and carried 6 guns. She carried the Mail, before the contract with the P. & O. Company.

No. 160. (*a*) AN OLD EAST INDIAMAN.

(*b*) P. & O. S. S. "Bentic."

(*c*) P. & O. S. S. "HINDUSTAN" (*Leaving Southampton, 24th September* 1842, *to open the Indian Mail Service*).

On the incorporation of the P. & O. Company in the year 1840, the Company constructed two vessels each of about 1,800 tons and 520 H. P. Two years later the East India Company entered into a contract with the P. & O. for a mail service between Calcutta, Suez, Madras and Ceylon, and on the 24th of September 1842, the S. S. "Hindustan" was despatched from Southampton to open the service in return for a subsidy of £115,000 a year.

No. 161. (*a*) AN EARLY GLIMPSE OF BOMBAY FROM THE HARBOUR.

(*b*) H. E. I. Co.'s CORVETTE "ELPHINSTONE."

(c) The Enterprise.

The decision to run steam ships to the East, resulted in the formation of a steam navigation company. Orders were given for building a steamship, to be named the "Enterprise." She was built at Deptford, and was of 470 tons burden and a nominal horse power of 120. She started under the command of Captain Johnson on August 16th, 1825, and after a voyage of 113 days, reached Calcutta. Her average speed was a little under nine knots. She was the first steamship to make the voyage to India.

No. 162. The East Indiaman "Swallow".

This was one of the ships built by the Wadias for the Indian Government. The vessel was about 700 tons and was armed with eighteen guns. She was launched in 1777, and was first used as a Company's Packet Boat, making several trips to England. She then joined the Bombay Marine, but shortly after returned to the packet service. In 1800, she was sold to the Danes, and proceeded to the West Indies, when she was seized by a British Man-of-War for breach of treaty and condemned as a prize. She was next purchased by the Admiralty and acted for several years as a war sloop. Later she became a merchant vessel and was finally lost on the "James and Mary" Shoal in the Hughli in 1823.

Miscellaneous Views of Bombay.

No. 163. GOVERNMENT HOUSE, MALABAR POINT, BOMBAY.

The present Government House is situated on the summit of Malabar Point. On this spot stood, about the year 1774, a lofty tower not far from the holy cleft named Sri Gundi. This was for some time the residence of the Peshwa Raghunathrao, and its ruins were seen by Mrs. Maria Graham in the year 1813. At first an occasional retreat of the Governor, General Medows, it became during the time of Sir E. Nepean, Governor of Bombay, from 1812 to 1819, the residence of the Governor of Bombay during the hottest part of the year. The Hon'ble Mountstuart Elphinstone erected a small bungalow, which has been described by Heber "as a very pretty cottage in a beautiful situation." Lady Falkland, wife of Viscount Falkland, Governor of Bombay, from 1848 to 1853, was very fond of Malabar Point, and during her residence in Bombay, she used to spend generally one or two hot seasons here. It continued to be partially occupied till the time of the Governorships of Lord Reay and Lord Harris, when it became the permanent residence of the Governor while in Bombay. The small bungalow was gradually enlarged, and many additions and alterations have since been made. H. R. H. The Prince of Wales (now H. M. King George V) resided here in the year 1905 when he visited the City. At present it consists of a number of bungalows, besides the residence of the Governor, and offices of the Private and Military Secretaries. It has an extensive and well kept garden.

No. 164. STATUARY OF BOMBAY.

(1) *Statue of Marquis of Wellesley.*

See note to No. 30.

This statue was executed by Chantrey, and was erected in the year 1814 by the merchants of Bombay as a "memorial of his wisdom, energy, and integrity." The statue originally stood near the site now occupied by the Queen's statue.

(2) *Statue of Lord Reay.*

See note to No. 87 (*e*).

This bronze statue of Lord Reay was modelled by the eminent sculptor Alfred Gilbert and erected by public subscription.

(3) *Statue of Lord Cornwallis.*

This statue was executed by Bacon and erected by public subcription after the death of Lord Cornwallis in the year 1805.

Lord Cornwallis (1738-1805) was the son of Charles, first Earl. He was eduacted at Eton. He entered the Guards in 1756 and was promoted to the rank of Major General in 1775. He served in the American War in 1776. He was appointed Governor-General of India in the 1786. He reformed both the civil and military services. In the year 1790, he took the command of the army against Tippoo of Mysore, and eventually succeeded in forcing him to surrender in 1792. He was created a Marquis in the same year. In the following year he announced the permanent settlement of the land revenue to be paid by the Zemindars in Bengal. In the 1793, he left India for England, and spent his time in military service on the continent. He was re-appointed Governor-General of India in 1805, but died shortly after his arrival in this country on the 5th of October 1805.

(4) *Statue of Mr. Justice M. G. Ranade.*

Mr. Ranade was born on January 20th, 1842. He received his education in the Elphinstone College, Bombay. He entered the British service in the year 1866 in the Educational Department. In the year 1868, he was appointed Acting Professor of English Literature in the Elphinstone College and remained there till 1871, when he was appointed Sub-Judge of Poona. In the year 1886 he was member of the Indian Finance Committee. Was several times member of the Bombay Legislative Council. He was appointed Judge of the Bombay High Court in the year 1893, and occupied the post till his death on January 17th 1901: The statue is the work of G. K. Mhatre of Bombay.

(5) *Statue of Sir R. Temple by Brock.*

See note to No. 87 (*c*).

(6) *Statue of Lord Sandhurst.*

See note to No. 88 (*b*).

No. 165. VIEW OF BOMBAY TAKEN FROM MALABAR HILL AT THE CLOSE OF THE 19TH CENTURY.

No. 166. DECORATIONS IN THE CITY AT THE TIME OF THE ROYAL VISIT IN THE YEAR 1911.

(*a*) *The Arch erected near the Bombay Municipal office.*

(*b*) *The Cotton Arch—Sandhurst Road.*

(*c*) *The Triumphal Arch at the Apollo Bundar.*

Royal Portraits.

No. 167. H. M. QUEEN VICTORIA.

Her Majesty Queen Victoria was born on May 24th, 1819. Ascended the throne on June 20th, 1837. Married on 10th February 1840, Albert, Prince of Saxe Coburg and Gotha. In the year 1876 "Empress of India" was added to the Royal Titles of Queen of England. The celebration of the jubilee of her reign in the year 1887 and ten years later of the diamond jubilee emphasised the loyalty of India and the colonies to the mother country. She died on January 22nd, 1901.

No. 168. H. M. KING GEORGE V.

H. M. King George V was born on 3rd June 1865, and succeeded his father H. M. the late King Edward VII in May 1910. In 1893 he married Princess Victoria Mary of Teck (now H. M. Queen Mary) the only daughter of H. H. the late Duke of Teck. As Prince and Princess of Wales they visited India in 1905, landing in Bombay on 5th November. Six years later he again came to India as King Emperor with H. M. the Queen Empress to announce his coronation to the Princes and people of India at the Imperial Durbar held at Delhi, which was henceforth declared to be the capital of India.

No. 169. H. M. QUEEN MARY.

See note to No. 168.

No. 170. GROUP TAKEN AT GOVERNMENT HOUSE, PAREL, BOMBAY, AT THE TIME OF THE VISIT OF H. M. THE LATE KING EDWARD VII AS PRINCE OF WALES IN NOVEMBER 1875.

No. 171. T. M. KING GEORGE AND QUEEN MARY AT THE APOLLO BUNDAR IN 1911.

No. 172. T. M. King George and Queen Mary receiving an address from the Bombay Municipal Corporation. The President reading the address.

No. 173. T. M. The King and Queen proceeding from the pavillion to the dais.

No. 174. T. M. leaving Apollo Bundar.

No. 175. H. M. King George reading his speech replying to the Municipal Address.

LIST OF BOOKS CONSULTED.

A true and exact description of the most celebrated East India Coasts of Malabar and Coromandel and also of the Isle of Ceylon, published in 1672. By P. Baldaeus.

Oriental Memoirs, published in 1813. By James Forbes, Esq.

The Indian Empire. By R. Montgomery, Esq.

Voyage from England to India, published in 1573. By E. Ives, Esq.

Indian Shipping, published in 1912. By Radhakumud Mookerji, Esq., M.A.

Life in Bombay and the Neighbouring Out-stations, published, in 1852. Anonymous.

The Byculla Club, published in 1916. By S. T. Sheppard, Esq.

Western India in 1838. By Mrs. Postans.

Description of a view of the Island and Harbour of Bombay published in 1831. By R. Burford.

The Origin of Bombay. By Dr. J. Gerson Da Cunha, M.R.C.S., L.M., etc.

Voyage to the East Indies, published in 1772. By M. Grose, Esq.

Chow-Chow, being selections of a Journal kept in India, Egypt and Syria, published in 1857. By Viscountess Falkland.

The Charm of Bombay, published in 1915. By R. P. Karkaria, Esq.

Encyclopedia Britannica, 9th Edition.

The Rise of Bombay, published in 1902. By S. M. Edwardes, Esq., I.C.S.

History of the Indian Navy, published in 1877. By C. R Low, Esq.

List of Pictures in Government House, Madras, published in 1903. By LT.-COL. H. D. LOVE, R.E.

The Portuguese in India, published in 1894. By F. C. DANVERS, ESQ.

The Old East Indiaman. By LT. K. CHATTERTON, R.N.V.R.

Dictionary of Indian Biography. By C. B. BUCKLAND, ESQ., C.I.E.

Gazetteer of the Bombay City and Island. By S. M. EDWARDES, ESQ., I.C.S.

Keigwin's Rebellion, published in 1916. By R. & O. STRACHEY.

The English in Western India, published in 1856. By P. ANDERSON, ESQ.

Bombay Place Names and Street Names, published in 1917. By S. T. SHEPPARD, ESQ.

Bombay and Western India, published in 1893. By J. DOUGLAS, ESQ.

Old and New Bombay. By G. CLARIDGE, ESQ.

The Indian Year Book, 1917.

Guide to Bombay, 1875. By J. M. MACLEAN, ESQ.

Scenery, Costumes and Architecture, chiefly on the Western side of India, published in 1830. By CAPT. R. M. GRINDLEY, M.R.A.S.

India Illustrated, published in 1826. By L. GILBERT, ESQ.

Materials towards a statistical account of the Town and Island of Bombay, 1894.